Memories of

Pontcysyllte

Memories of

Pontcysyllte

Amy Douglas and Fiona Collins

TEMPUS

Frontispiece: *Bicentenary celebrations of the opening of the aqueduct, Trevor Basin, 26 November 2005. (Ed Fisher)*

First published 2006

Tempus Publishing Limited
The Mill, Brimscombe Port,
Stroud, Gloucestershire, GL5 2QG

British Library Cataloguing in Publication Data.
A catalogue record for this book is available from the British Library.

ISBN 0 7524 3770 4

Typesetting and origination by Tempus Publishing Limited
Printed in Great Britain

Contents

Preface

The waters run still, the waters run deep.
These stories are yours, for you to keep.

Still waters run deep, or so they say. The waters of the river Dee, *yr afon Dyfrdwy*, run still and deep, turbulent and wild, as they flow out to the sea from their source in the mountains of western Wales. These waters have formed the landscape of the Vale of Llangollen into a bowl: a fertile, sheltered valley where humans have lived since the earliest times. Humans have worked on the land, and also under the land, digging out the stone and clay and coal they need, using the gifts of the land, and using the water too. It was Thomas Telford who drew the waters out of the river, at Horseshoe Falls, and channelled them into the Llangollen Canal, for human use in commerce and industry. He carried them across the valley on the Pontcysyllte Aqueduct – *the bridge that connects*, the 'river that runs in the sky'. This book is a collection of stories from the people who live all around the aqueduct: in Acrefair, Cefn Mawr, Froncysyllte, Garth, Newbridge, Pentre, Rhosymedre and Trevor. They are stories of love, life, loss and laughter.

This is not the first time that the area around the aqueduct has featured in a book of memories. In 1854 George Borrow began an epic walk around Wales, which was to result in the publication of his book *Wild Wales*. In it, he recalled a walk along the canal from Llangollen to Froncysyllte Basin, in the company of John Jones, a local shepherd. When they crossed the aqueduct, which Borrow described as 'this mighty bridge', Borrow and John Jones stared dizzily down over the side at the river Dee below, and agreed that it made their heads spin. Borrow recorded John Jones' words: 'This is the Pontcysyllte, sir. It's the finest bridge in the world, and no wonder, if what the common people say be true, namely that every stone cost a golden sovereign.' We hope you'll agree that the stories collected here, and the people who told us these stories, are worth their weight in gold.

Amy Douglas and Fiona Collins
December 2005

Acknowledgements

We would like to thank everyone involved with the Voices Around the Aqueduct project who has given time, support and enthusiasm; this book would not exist without you.

In particular we would like to thank the following:

The funders of the project:
European Union Leader +
Northern Marches Cymru
WDA
Wrexham County Borough Council

Members of the project's steering group:
Liz Carding, Senior Ranger, Wrexham County Borough Council Parks, Countryside and Rights of Way Service
Joanna Finch, Education and Heritage Ranger, Wrexham County Borough Council Parks, Countryside and Rights of Way Service
Karen Harris, Community Development Officer, Northern Marches Cymru
Martin Howorth, Parks, Countryside and Rights of Way Manager, Wrexham County Borough Council
Barbara Lloyd Jones, History Coordinator, Cefn Mawr County Primary School
Kris Morrison, Cefn, Rhosymedre and Newbridge Community Association
Iola Roberts, Llangollen Rural Community Council
Joy Thomas, Local Studies Librarian, Wrexham Heritage Services

Members of the following community groups:
Acrefair Community Association
Acrefair Senior Citizens' Group
Acrefair Youth Club
Cefn Past and Present Local History Group
First Acrefair Brownie Pack
Froncysyllte Darby and Joan Club
Froncysyllte Male Voice Choir/Cor Meibion Froncysyllte
The Venue After School Club, Plas Madoc
Tŷ Mawr Country Park Junior Rangers

Headteachers, staff and pupils of the following schools:
Acrefair Primary School
Cefn Mawr County Primary School
Froncysyllte County Primary School
Garth County Primary School
Pentre Church in Wales School
Rhosymedre Infants' School
Rhosymedre Junior School
Ysgol Min-y-Ddol

Staff of the following local services:
Alasdair Thomson at Alyn Waters Country Park
Joy Thomas and Kevin Plant at the A.N. Palmer Centre for Local Studies and Archives
Tracey Roberts and her colleagues at Bod Llwyd Care Home
Howard Griffiths at British Waterways Board
Sue Evans and her team at Cefn Community Café
Vicky Williams and her colleagues at Cefn Mawr Library
Hannah Jones, Anna Pollard and their team at Groundwork Wrexham and Flintshire
Liz, Jo, Bill, Karen, Kia, Sue, Claire, Tracey and Stuart at Tŷ Mawr Country Park
Vikki Reynolds at Wrexham Arts Centre

Staff of the following local industries:
Hazel Harvey at Air Products PLC
John R. Ferrari, Senior Mechanical Engineer at Flexsys Rubber Chemicals Ltd
Myk at The Bakery

Individuals:
Mike Gleed
Glyn Jones
Monica Jones
Ian Parry
Nance Rogers
Joyce Upton

Introduction

The villages of Acrefair, Cefn Mawr, Froncysyllte, Garth, Newbridge, Pentre, Rhosymedre and Trevor surround the river Dee, *yr afon Dyfrdwy*, in Wrexham County Borough, North Wales. They were once thriving industrial communities. The industrial activity was based upon the extraction of the local natural resources and a wide range of associated manufacturing industries: coal mines, stone quarries, limestone works, ironworks, terracotta potteries and chemical works.

In the late eighteenth century it was proposed to link this rich industrial area with the ports of Liverpool and Bristol and the markets of Britain by means of canal navigation. In 1805 Thomas Telford opened the Pontcysyllte Aqueduct, carrying the canal at a height of 121ft over the river Dee. This is widely recognised as an amazing feat of engineering and a beautiful and awe-inspiring feature in the Vale of Llangollen. The name of the aqueduct translates as 'the bridge that connects'.

In 2005 the aqueduct was 200 years old. Wrexham County Borough Council, in partnership with British Waterways, Northern Marches Cymru, local industries and community groups set up a programme of events and projects to celebrate the bicentenary. This book is the outcome of one of these projects.

Voices Around the Aqueduct was a project created by storytellers Amy Douglas and Fiona Collins. They worked with community groups, schools, senior citizens' clubs and individuals to create a celebration of the past, present and future of these local communities. Leading up to the celebrations for the bicentenary of the opening of Pontcysyllte Aqueduct on 26 November 2005, the project focused on ordinary people and their extraordinary lives.

The storytellers spent nine months collecting old memories, young memories, anecdotes, jokes, tall tales and wistful moments from people living in the villages all around the aqueduct. A storytelling performance entitled *Still Waters Run Deep* was created from these stories and presented to the local communities during November 2005.

This book brings these memories to a wider audience. It is a collection of oral recollections, personal memories and photographs gathered over the years. All the stories were recorded during conversations and interviews, then transcribed. We hope you will be able to hear the sound of the different voices speaking as you read these transcripts.

Everyone remembers events from their own point of view. Every effort has been made to give a balanced picture of life in the villages, but it has been difficult to condense all the material into one volume. These are the stories of the people who live all around the aqueduct, told in their own voices.

Amy Douglas tells stories from the memory box to children from Ysgol Min y Ddol. (Liz Carding)

Fiona Collins leads a storywalk from Tŷ Mawr to the aqueduct. (Anna Pollard)

List of Contributors

Sonia T. Benbow-Jones
Pauline (Polly) Bluck
Liz Carding
Warren Coleman
Bill Davies
Mair Davies Jones
H. Cecil Diggory
Patricia Joan Diggory
Dorothy Edwards
Tom Evans
Gwyneth Feathers
Ed Fisher
Pete Garrett
Eluned Griffiths
Neil Hayward-Fraser
Mary Hughes
Arthur Humphreys
Barbara Humphreys
Betty James
Ann Jones
Ben Jones
Betty Jones
Edward Jones
Gertrude Jones
Lydia Jones
Moyra Kempster
Brenda Little
Joe Little
Kris Morrison

Audrey Owens
Howard Paddock
Diane Parry
Gwyneth Partington
Gladys Peters
Anna Pollard
Diane Powell
Vikki Reynolds
Edna Roberts
Emrys Roberts
Gary Roberts
Iola Roberts
Margaret Roberts
Rhona Roberts
David Russell Roberts
Maggie Saunders
Kathleen Smith
Hilary Spragg
Betty Thompson
Alasdair Thomson
Marjorie Tod
Bob Watkin
Dennis Williams
Janet Williams
Julie Williams
Vaughan Williams
Karen Wright
Olwen Wright
Peter Wright

one

Childhood

The great Dee viaduct, from The Illustrated London News *of 21 October 1848. (Howard Paddock)*

Howard's birth

I've lived here all my life. I was born in Mount Pleasant. If you go on to the BBC North Wales website there's a poem of mine there, 'A blue flag was flown'. It relates to when I was born in 1944: my father was a railway man, he was working on the viaduct, and as a signal that the baby had been born they put a sheet on the washing line, in the garden:

> *'Twas in forty four on the tenth of May*
> *That I was born at the family home.*
> *A railway worker, my father that day*
> *Was in sight of our house and would not roam.*
> *To signal my birth a blue flag was flown*
> *For the workers to see was their intent,*
> *Proud father was cheered, his trumpet was blown*
> *And lots of flowers to my mother sent.*

Howard Paddock, born 1944

Pat Collins' birth

I'll just tell you about Pat Collins' fair, used to be on the bank. Mrs Collins went into labour, with Pat Collins, and they couldn't get her to the hospital quick enough, she was in the caravan, on the bank ... so he was born there. Every March they came, the March Fair was there, and all the classes from school used to go up in the afternoon, and he would put the fair on for us all to have a free ride, because he was born here, old Pat Collins.

Gertrude Jones, born 1915

Mary's birth

[I have a] Welsh translation of *Pilgrim's Progress*: it belonged to my great great grandfather Jonathon Powell. It's been used more or less as people use a family Bible, with Jonathan and all his offspring in the back, starting off with him – well actually, it's only got his first wife, and the children they had. It shows how very into his chapel he was, because at the bottom it's got written in Welsh: 'Mary Powell, born April 10th 1864, on the Sunday that A.J. Parry preached at the funeral service of Dr Evans, at Seion, Cefn Mawr.' That seemed equally important as the fact that he'd got another

Joshua Powell and his eldest daughter, Sarah Anne, from his first marriage. (Diane Powell)

The Aqueduct inn. (Emrys Roberts)

daughter. Seven children, and out of those, I don't know about Anne, she was still alive at twenty, but with the exception of Joshua, who was my great-grandfather, the others all died before their fourth birthday.

Diane Powell, born 1946

Birthday parties

I was born in the Aqueduct Inn, my grandparents kept it from 1927 to 1938, so I was brought up in a pub. The good times were all my birthday parties: they'd cover the snooker table and lay out all the food with a lovely big birthday cake. Yes, it was a happy childhood in Fron.

Dennis Williams, born 1931

Oak Ball Day

29th May is Oak Ball Day,
If we don't have a holiday,
We'll all run away!

Dennis Williams with his mother Harriet and his father Roger, c. 1934. (Dennis Williams)

We always had a half-day holiday from [Acrefair] school on Oak Ball Day, 29 May. We used to chant this, not to the teachers, because they knew we were having a holiday, but it was just a chant in the schoolyard. We'd go to the oak trees to find the oak balls and then bring them to school to show.

Betty Thompson, born 1922, and other members of Acrefair Senior Citizens' Group

Members of Acrefair Senior Citizens' Group talking about the past to schoolchildren of today. (Vikki Reynolds)

Gloria Meller

I remember the wall at the side [of Acrefair School], where we used to push each other off – we used to play King of the Castle on the wall. Outside toilets, we used to have to go up the yard for the toilets. We'd have days off in the winter because the toilets would be frozen. We used to play rounders on the top part of the yard and see whoever could get the ball to go over the school. There was only one who ever did it – Gloria Meller – she got the ball to go right over the school, nobody else did it.

Diane Parry, born 1944

Miss Jones

There was a Miss Jones at Acrefair at the time; she was elderly, used to wear these crossover pinnies. She put a plaster on his mouth, this boy Terry, for being naughty, and she also put a placard round his neck. I remember

thinking how awful it was then – can you imagine it now?

Diane Parry, born 1944

School canteen

The Community Hall in Acrefair was the school canteen. I used to come home for dinner and it was quite a treat if I was allowed to stay for school dinners. If my mum was going out anywhere, I used to stay. And I seem to remember, if it was snowy or icy I used to stay as well. I remember that canteen being built.

Diane Powell, born 1946

Going to school

I always remember going to school. I heard the children playing in Cefn School and I walked down and I went into class and I sat down with them. I was three and everybody was looking for me and I was in school. I remember being brought back again.

Gwyneth Partington, born 1919

Slate and sand

We had quite a happy childhood. There were six of us. My father worked in the brickworks. Five of us went to Cefn School; my eldest

An aerial photograph of Acrefair School, published by Aerofilms Ltd. (Edward Jones)

sister went to Rhosymedre. We used to walk to school; there were no cars. I can remember my first day at school, and the teacher was Mrs Hurst. She'd got a long black skirt down to her feet and black buttoned boots with a white lace bodice, real old-fashioned, you know. The schools then in Cefn were different from what they are today. There was the girls' school, and the infants' in the middle, and the boys' school on the other side. They all had their own yards; [boys and girls] didn't mix at all, only in the infants. It was all brick inside as well, the classrooms were painted dark red at the top and dark green at the bottom and the windows were high, so you couldn't see out, and no one could see in. It was further along than where the schools are now, going towards Queen Street in Cefn. There was a big fireplace in the corner, with a big bucket of coal, and in the winter, when it was very cold, we had to leave our coats on because we were so cold. I can remember, when we started to write, we were given a slate with sand on it and as the teacher put the letters on the board, we had to make the letter in the sand and she would come around and inspect what we'd done.

Betty James, born 1922

Milk and cod liver oil

The good times we had marching down to the canteen [at Cefn School]! The canteen was in the lower field and we all marched down in order to the canteen, which was a separate building at the far end of the playing field, still there today. The dinners were great: plenty of fresh vegetables, rice pudding, fruit pie and custard. We enjoyed them so much we used to queue up for seconds. And of course we had milk, had your bottle of milk in the mornings. In the infant school we used to have a sleep in the afternoon, two o'clock they let you have a sleep on your own little mattress and the teacher gave you a little bottle of orange with cod liver oil in it, every day. It was good for you. I don't think it would be appreciated today.

David Russell Roberts, born 1944

Missing sister

There were four of us sisters and we were all in Cefn School at the same time. I was the oldest, then Moyra, then Margaret, then Pat. There was a little nursery down the bottom where they used to put the very young ones to bed in the afternoon. We were in the top school and then our youngest sister down there. Nearly every afternoon she'd go missing or screaming. The teacher would come up and say, 'Your sister's gone missing' because she wouldn't go to bed. She went home one day, she walked all the way to Cae Goch on her own. I can remember that, because Moyra and I went looking for her. Because it was bedtime, they had flat wooden beds, I think she had the idea in her mind that she was there staying. She must have been, what, three and a half. She thought bedtime was bedtime and she should have been at home, not staying in school. She wouldn't have it!

Edna Roberts, born 1936

A war hero

Cefn School was quite a big school, both infants and the junior. I enjoyed all my days at Cefn School; they were good times, good days. The headmaster, Mr Williams at that time, was very good and Mr Raymond Arthur was another excellent teacher who lived in the area. He played the piano for school concerts and for various choirs in the area. He was known as a war hero. He had a limp. He had injured his leg as a pilot in the war. He was a great teacher. Mr Arthur and Mr Williams were the two that stick in my mind apart from Miss E. Barrick, who was the only lady teacher in the boys' school.

David Russell Roberts, born 1944

Lizzie Bach

We had a lady teacher, she was Welsh, Lizzie Bach, we used to call her. She was a rum 'un. She was a bloomin' rum 'un, I tell you! There was no messing with her, no messing at all. I said to myself, I'll have to behave meself this morning, because she was like that. Well, I suppose with a lot of children, you can imagine how we were! She used to froth at the mouth, oh, I can see her now! I remember Lizzie Bach used to stand by the fire with her skirt up... She had the cane, many a time I've been up for the cane. I'd pull my hand away, then hold it out again – you had to have it. Hard times, for the children!

Bill Davies, born 1912

Headteacher Hannaby

I started my education at Fron Schools in 1927. I use the term 'schools' loosely because at that time there were two separate schools in the village. Although they were located on the same site, the infants' school had its own headteacher, Miss M.C. Williams, and she was assisted by her sister, Miss M.F. Williams. This school catered for children up to age seven, when they transferred to the separate junior school. The headteacher of the junior school at the time was Mr Herbert Hannaby, whose staff comprised of six assistant teachers. Mr Hannaby and his staff imparted an education which provided a good foundation for adult life. They were a group of dedicated teachers whose head was a strict disciplinarian. From a personal point of view, he knocked some sense into me and pointed me in the right direction for my future life. His strict discipline didn't affect me too greatly as my father was also a rather strict person who suffered little nonsense at all so it was not a great problem for me. At that time, great stress was laid on neat handwriting in the school. The headteacher had the gift of beautiful handwriting and I think he and his staff tried to get us all to emulate him.

Emrys Roberts, born 1922

Dennis Williams presents John Prescott, a former pupil of Froncysyllte School, with a Froncysyllte Male Voice Choir CD, watched by John's mother, 2000. (Dennis Williams)

Respect

I used to go, years ago, to Fron School. When we were in Fron School, the headmaster there was Mr Hannaby. But I think today the respect has gone. We thought he was a wonderful man but we were petrified of him. He'd give you the cane but you'd still respect him.

Audrey Owens, born 1938

Emrys Roberts (in front of the curate) in St David's church choir, 1929. (Emrys Roberts)

A big black stove

When I started [Froncysyllte] school, lighting was by means of oil lamps but in 1929 a mains gas supply was laid on to the village by the Cefn and District Gas Company and the school was connected up. This was followed up within a short time by a new electricity supply which came to the village. Heating of the classrooms was by means of a big black stove fuelled by coke, which the boys used to have to take it in turns to bring up in buckets from the cellar. Originally, we sat in rather long desks – I think there were four to a desk – which had a hinged seat and the desk top was equipped with four of the old-fashioned ceramic inkwells.

Emrys Roberts, born 1922

The three Rs

In [Froncysyllte] school you had to learn sewing and knitting and things like this. The main thing, though, was the three Rs. We used to know the times tables backwards; the children don't today, do they? We used to do them over and over and over again.

Betty Jones, born 1938

First assistant cook

There were no school meals at the time I was in Fron School. I think the school meals service started in Fron in the early 1940s – I was abroad at the time. My mother was the first assistant cook at the school, with Mrs Jones from Penygraig Farm as the cook.

Emrys Roberts, born 1922

Passing the scholarship

There was a scholarship at that time, the eleven-plus. The headmaster always took the scholarship class [at Froncysyllte School]. There'd be perhaps half a dozen in the scholarship class. You had to be good: if they didn't think you'd pass, you wouldn't be in the class. It was always nearly a 100 per cent pass rate. I can remember when I passed the scholarship, the results came to school and then they'd allow you home to tell your parents – it was the middle of the day, you know. Now Mrs Jones was a lovely person, she lived by the Co-op and she saw us running down the village; the school's on the top of the village and our house was below the main road, at the side of the canal. She said, 'Oh, you've passed the scholarship, have you? You tell the others all to come here on the way back after school.' She gave us all a shilling each for passing the scholarship.

Betty Jones, born 1938

Freezing in the winter

Rhosymedre Church School had got quite a good name for its teaching and was one of the first schools in the area. In the 1960s it closed and the new schools were built nearer to Plas Madoc. I'm chair of the governing body of one of them. This was a church school, now used as a church centre. The church came first and the school followed after. That's where I went to school and then I went on to Ruabon Grammar School, the girls' school, which was separate then from the boys' school. Freezing in the winter!

Rhona Roberts, born 1928

Breaking school windows

I remember breaking the school windows, of course, with balls or stones. My father was a joiner; he used to follow me round replacing the glass! Because of that I always seemed to get the fault.

David Russell Roberts, born 1944

Getting the cane

Mr Williams used to have a cane in Cefn School. If he caught you climbing on the shelters – there were the old air-raid shelters there with concrete roofs – and if he saw you climbing on those to fetch your ball, he was very strict in that respect and you'd get the cane and that stung: a big rap on the back of the knuckles or seven of the best on your backside.

David Russell Roberts, born 1944

Size ten plimsoll

I never got the cane, I never got that bad! Nobody had the cane in the junior school. It was in the senior school [Acrefair Secondary Modern]. They would get Mr Callas, he was the maths teacher and he'd a big plimsoll, size ten, and anybody was out of order he would give them a bash with this big plimsoll. Some of the boys would get the stick in the senior school, but the girls didn't.

Diane Parry, born 1944

Stanier-class JMT 4-6-0 No. 45031 at Ruabon station, looking from the south, 1965. (Pete Garrett)

Size twelve plimsoll

In Ruabon School the French lesson was the worst – the teacher used to have a long, size twelve plimsoll, very, very thin, he didn't use a stick, he used a plimsoll with a large sole and, by gum, did that sting. You were jumping around the classroom for ten minutes after having that. I don't know whether that was because I was bad in French or what, but that really is vivid in my mind. Perhaps not taking the interest I should in a French lesson. Didn't do any of us any harm though. Did us all good in the long run.

David Russell Roberts, born 1944

The Marchwiel train

When I was in Ruabon Grammar School, I and others could come home on what was called the Marchwiel train. This was a train put on to take workers from the Ordnance Factory home. The cost was three halfpence, pre-decimal money.

Rhona Roberts, born 1928

Semolina and strawberry jam

Even in [Ruabon] grammar school we had fantastic meals. We had a prefect head of the dining table, six up either side, and he'd distribute the food out of hot metal containers – all fresh vegetables and meat, lovely. I'd never grumble about school meals. Not even semolina and strawberry jam!

David Russell Roberts, born 1944

Regrets

My father lost his leg in the pit, so of course he didn't work. So my mother said, 'Well, I can't afford two of you in grammar school.' And then it was the policy that the boys, they were the ones that would go. So she said, 'Your brother will have to go.' I was the oldest but he would have to go. So he passed and he went. But I always remember him calling me, Mr Hannaby, and he said, 'The point is, Audrey, you've come to what we can teach you here. I suggest that you go to the Central School at Acrefair which will advance your studies.' Well, that didn't cost nothing, but the only thing was that you had to walk there, over the aqueduct! It was wonderful there, the headmaster was Mr Bowen and he was a wonderful man. I enjoyed my time there but I always regret I never went to grammar school but that's how things were then. All I'm thankful for today is that my brother did very well. He was a professor. He's in Australia now, he's retired, but he was a professor in Canada, Hong Kong and everywhere, so he did well for himself.

Audrey Owens, born 1938

We were foreign

It was very hard because we were foreign. I can remember in school at the time of the Hungarian uprising being asked to explain the background and actually thinking what a horrible lot of people they were. And they actually made me stand up and give a historical background to the uprising and we weren't Hungarian, we were Polish. I asked my parents about this and then went back and told the class.

Sonia T. Benbow-Jones, born 1943

More Welsh

They did more advanced learning and there was much more Welsh going on in the schools than there is now. I always remember my brother saying when he went to the school of languages in London they said because you can speak Welsh, you can learn any language, because Welsh, they reckon, is one of the most difficult, worst languages to learn.

Audrey Owens, born 1938

Less Welsh

All my father's family were Welsh-speaking but my mother came from Oldham. Mind you, in the first part of the twentieth century, it wasn't popular to teach your children [Welsh], it was considered it would hold you back.

Howard Paddock, born 1944

Welsh Not

Gwyneth: I went to Cefn school. We didn't have much Welsh there. It was almost discouraged. Well, it wasn't all that long after the Welsh Not, was it? My grandfather was there when the Welsh Not was being given. We learnt to sing in Welsh and had recitation. We did have Welsh, in Cefn, but it wasn't encouraged, even though the head, Miss Turner, was Welsh. I never remember having Welsh lessons. We were taught to sing and we had bits of Eisteddfodau and things but we weren't taught Welsh.

Edward: I was taught in English and we were encouraged not to speak Welsh, to encourage the evacuees.

Gwyneth: When you went to Ruabon, if you came from Cefn, you did French. If you came from Rhos, you did Welsh. They didn't encourage you to learn it.

Edward Jones, born 1937, Mair Davies Jones, born 1928, Gwyneth Partington, born 1919 (Cefn Past and Present Group)

Penillion

I changed school and went to secondary in Acrefair. I'd never sung in Welsh and they spoke Welsh in this school, so I did my Welsh with an English/Welsh dictionary and I sat the exams like that, but I could sing in Welsh because I didn't know what I was singing! And that's when I first learnt Penillion singing – you sing one tune and the harp or piano plays a different one. I won in the school Eisteddfod competition on St David's Day.

Sonia T. Benbow-Jones, born 1943

Denny Wet-leg

Coming to school, we used to come along the canal and check our nightlines. The only things we caught at nighttime were eels, because for some reason they come out at night. And you'd go along in the morning and see what you'd caught and it would always be an eel. Inevitably I would fall in the canal and get one leg wet. Everybody had nicknames. So I was Denny Wet-leg.

Dennis Williams, born 1931

Adventure playground

On Rock Road there used to be some prefabs and at the back there was a quarry which hadn't been working, it was an adventure playground for us, a great place to mess about in.

Pete Garrett, born 1949

Pocket money

I used to have a sixpence a week. It was tuppence to go into the matinee in Cefn. There were two cinemas there and we used to like Westerns and Captain Marvel and stuff like that. And then it was tuppence for the bus and it left you with a penny or tuppence and we used to club together and buy a loaf. And say there were five of you, we'd break it with our bare hands and we'd eat that while we were waiting for the bus.

Edward Jones, born 1937

First television

Margaret: We had the first television around here, a little one.

Gary: It was only a little tiny one. It was nine inches by nine inches, I think, that's all it was.

Margaret: Muffin the Mule was on, they'd all come, four o'clock after school and they'd all say, 'Is it on, Auntie Margaret?' 'Yes, come on'. They'd all walk in, all sit on the floor, all round. My husband was on tankers, for Monsanto.

Gary: He couldn't come in his own house!

Margaret: He would call to put his bag ready to go down, he'd be stepping over them and the bags of chips we'd make in little cones for them. When it was over, they'd all say thank you and traipse out. It was like a picture palace!

Gary: When it first came, you see, a lot of people hadn't got TV. There was gas but there was no electric in some places.

Margaret Roberts, born 1919, and Gary Roberts, born 1945

The railway children

We'd seen the Jenny Agutter series on television, *The Railway Children*. That must have been in the '50s when that first came out. The way our house is, our land is higher than the start of the house at the bottom. Mummy and Daddy were very keen for us to live outside as much as we could in the nice weather. In the summer, the table was out there, the chairs were out there, we'd be out there in our pyjamas waiting for Mr Evans the milkman to deliver the milk, with our cornflakes and our big pot of tea and when the trains went past we used to wave to them because we were convinced we were the railway children!

Sonia T. Benbow-Jones, born 1943

Blocked with snow

I went to school in Wrexham, so I got the train to Wrexham and my brothers and sisters were in school in Cefn so they would go before me and they would go down Plas Kynaston Lane, the other side of the railway bridge, and I'd be on the train and we'd be waving to each other as I was going into school in Wrexham. Many's the time I'd be running out the house late, with my breakfast in my hand

Rock Road, Rhosymedre, showing the prefabs where Llys-y-craig is now. (Arthur and Barbara Humphries)

The view towards Garth Mountain. (Dennis Williams)

and the steam train would come up, they'd see me coming out the house and they would be going as slow as they can from the bridge to the railway station, as I'd be running up the hill as quick as I can to get the train. The road used to get blocked with the snow in the winter but the steam trains would still come through. The Wrexham side was the far side of the railway tracks so you had to go over the railway bridge to the waiting room and it had a big pot-bellied stove and what we used to do was bring wood in and light the fire when we were waiting for the train because it was so cold. Even though the stationmaster told us not to light a fire we wanted to be warm whilst we waited for the train. You'd go into the waiting room and there'd be ice on the inside of the window. So that was fun. And that's all '50s, early '60s.

Sonia T. Benbow-Jones, born 1943

Making sledges

We used to look forward to the winters. I remember 1947 was a bad winter and up Garth we loved the winter because you could go sledging on the road. You could get on your sledge there at the top of Garth by a place called Gronwen, and if the road conditions were right you could go all the way to Trevor, by the Australia Arms. We used to make all our own sledges. They were made of wood, like Swiss toboggans. They used to have these old-fashioned beds, with poles on them, and lengths of steel reinforcing these beds, and they made ideal runners. So you'd take these and sort of pin them. They would be on wooden runners and you would polish them, so they were polished steel on the road. That's what we used for sledges.

Edward Jones, born 1937

Making do

Edna: And then sometimes we couldn't go [to school] because of the snow. You'd have that much snow you wouldn't be able to go.

Moyra: We used to go down the bank. Well, we never had a sledge.

Edna: We had corrugated sheets of metal, anything.

Moyra: An old mat or something.

Edna: And because we were high up, you could go right the way down. We'd go down from where we were on the little hill, just a bit along and down the steep hill, which was Seion Hill, a turn, straight the way down to the main road and straight over the road to Monsanto and past Monsanto. But there wasn't so much traffic then, was there?

Moyra: We weren't supposed to have gone where we went, mind.

Edna: All children are the same though, aren't they, you're told not to and you do it.

Edna Roberts, born 1936, and Moyra Kempster, born 1938

Worst earhole

I tell you when I had the worst earhole. We had some red cabbage in the allotment, I didn't know, for show. We had to go down there one day for two, three hours. We were looking at this red cabbage. I had a stick and I said, 'I'll be first.' I was clacking them with a stick. And they all bursted! And I was bursted and all! Life was poor, but it was great.

Bill Davies, born 1912

They knew who you were

Edna: The worst thing you did was knock people's doors and run away. And then we used to put paper up the drainpipe and then light the paper so it would make like a lion's roar.

Moyra: Tie the string to the knocker, go and hide and then pull the string and they'd come to the door and you wouldn't be there.

Edna: They knew who you were though.

Moyra: It would always be our house. If anything was going on it was No. 2. That would be the first house they would make for.

Edna: Or someone had a couple of apple trees, you'd pinch a couple of apples. And we got caught. They would come round and that would be it. My father never hit us; he never smacked us or anything. My mother did but my father only had to raise his voice and that was it, you knew then you were in trouble. But that's all we used to do.

Edna Roberts, born 1936, and Moyra Kempster, born 1938

B-flat tenor trombone

I always wanted to play a brass instrument, so when I was at college I played B-flat tenor trombone. I used to stand by the yew tree going up to the top garden when they were in Cefn Bychan Chapel and practise 'Abide With Me', which would reverberate in the bridge when they were in the chapel. I was a lovely child!

Sonia T. Benbow-Jones, born 1943

Poor Bill

We had a little raft on the canal, with two drums tied together with rope and planks on the top. We were playing on it and then we realised that my mate Bill Evans was coming from chapel. So we had the grand idea of loosening the ropes and getting him to go on it, and as it got to the centre it would part. He got on the raft and we pushed him out, and when it was in the middle of the canal the raft started coming apart. You could see on Bill's face that he knew we had set him up, as he quietly disappeared into the water in his best Sunday suit.

Dennis Williams, born 1931

Above: *Dennis, Iris, Len and Hazel Williams, during Len's naughty phase. (Dennis Williams)*

Left: *Len and Hazel Williams walking up to Fron from the swing bridge. (Dennis Williams)*

Came out coughing

Patricia: Who were the people that had a boat there, with a fire and a grate and a chimney, and you went and put slates on the top of it, and they all came out coughing?

Cecil: We did some soft things, as kids.

Patricia: Were they canal people?

Cecil: No, I don't think they were. They were fellows working on it, carrying clay, I think, and they lived in the back end of it.

Patricia Diggory, born 1924, and Cecil Diggory, born 1920

Water and lime

We used to fill bottles with water and lime to try to blow up the fish, but it never worked. You'd shake the bottle, put the top back on, and drop it in the canal. It would explode, but we never got any fish.

Dennis Williams, born 1931

Len the terror

I've got a little brother, and he was a terror. It was firework night and the next day we were all getting up in the morning. It was an old-fashioned house with the chimney and coal fire. The next thing, there was an almighty explosion. Len had thrown a dud firework from the night before onto the fire and it had gone off, and the soot of about ten years had come down. When we got to school, my sisters they were all like miners, where the soot still stays after you've had a wash. They couldn't get it off. So I came home that night and mother said, 'You'd better go and find him.' He hadn't come home, he was afraid to. So I went off. I knew where to find him, he was underneath the aqueduct, under the bridge with his mates. So I had to walk all the way to the aqueduct bridge to bring him home for his punishment. We had a nice orchard in Tŷ Uchaf, quite a lot of trees and my Dad was getting quite upset because there were some lads stealing his apples.

We could see the hole in the hedge where they were coming in. He said, 'I'll get them tonight.' So I went there with my Dad, we could see them coming, we could hear them whispering, coming down. Anyway, the first lad came through and my Dad grabbed him. But what a surprise — it was my brother!

Dennis Williams, born 1931

Pen-y-wal

There were policemen about but you had respect for the policemen. Mr Roberts, he lived across the road in that house there and we'd be standing on Pen-y-wal at the end of the wall. He'd come along, we'd all jump down. I can see him now. He'd have his truncheon in his hand, and he'd speak to you: 'Right, you know what I want, no one here when I get back.' He never seemed to have that much trouble.

Audrey Owens, born 1938

two

Pastimes

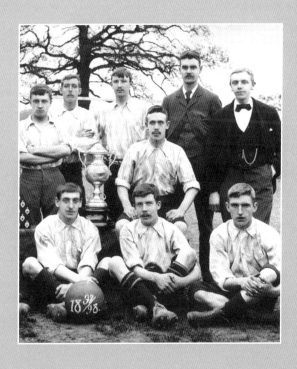

The cinemas

A lot of people remember the Palace. It was a shilling in the balcony and sixpence downstairs. It was more or less a corrugated building, if I remember it rightly, and there was a terrific lot of steps. My Dad knew John Owen, as we called him, who was the owner. My father didn't drink but he used to go up and see John Owen, and he'd come home sometimes and he'd start to laugh and we'd say, 'What's up?' Well, there were always mischievous lads in those days and if the film got a bit exciting, or it slowed down, they used to bang their feet and John Owen used to rush up and down with a flashlight and it used to amuse my father because as soon as he shone his light somewhere, it'd stop. How daft can you get?

Kathleen Smith, born 1923

The Palace theatre in the 1930s, before it burnt down. (Arthur and Barbara Humphries)

Mr Jones

We used to get the bus to the pictures and it was amazing, you used to be queuing down the Cefn Hill there. There was Old Hall at the top and the Palace at the bottom, you'd be queuing all the way down the street. And then you couldn't get a bus home unless you came out the pictures early, so of course you'd walk home, and that was the time you met up with the lads. You weren't allowed to go until you were about fifteen, until you were working and you'd got your own money. I always remember being in the Palace, the one down the steps, and we were all sitting in the front row. And you know how you were then, somebody had got a cigarette and of course everyone was smoking along the row. And this old man used to come round, Mr Jones would come with the torch, and he was flashing the torch, trying to make them put out the cigarette. I mean it never tacked on to me, I didn't like it, but that was when a lot of people started, from then. You weren't supposed to be smoking at that age. He'd be coming up and down the aisle with that torch.

Audrey Owens, born 1938

Ballroom dancing

We used to dance a lot, my husband and I. I couldn't be bothered looking at another man. Fifty-odd years, we were married. I loved him to bits. Ballroom dancing – waltzes, tangos, slow foxtrots – none of this sort of jiving. There was a good place to dance in Wrexham, with a band. It used to be over Burton's. I had a favourite grey skirt and a red top I used to like.

Dolly Edwards, born 1915

Skylighting

In Llangollen, in the Town Hall, they used to have dances. I remember going there

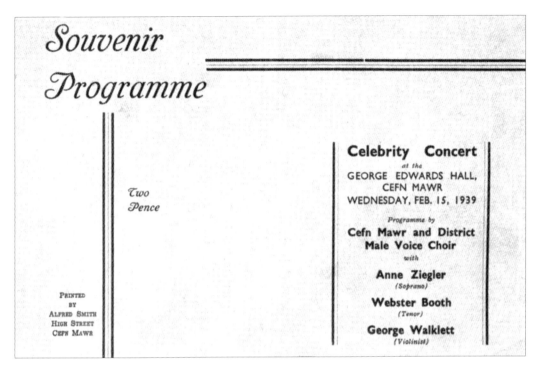

A celebrity concert souvenir programme. (Mary Hughes)

as I got older. This one time I remember, they wouldn't let these lads in so three of them climbed up the roof and got in the skylight.

Audrey Owens, born 1938

Celebrity concerts

Anne Ziegler and Webster Booth, they were husband and wife, he came first on his own and then the next year they came together. He was a prime tenor. We had a lot of concerts. We usually had a celebrity and a local, but those were top notch. David Lloyd ... was the Welsh top notch. The interesting thing is that the accompanist for these people, Maelor Richards, he had a deformity. He was the official accompanist for the celebrity concerts. He was a very, very good musician. Amazingly, these top class people that were coming from London and from everywhere else, he'd play

for them. No practice at all. He might run over it for ten minutes, whatever they brought he would just play. At that time I would be in the George Edwards Hall. I'd play for the choir, come off stage, go down the side with the choir and he'd go and play for the soloist. There'd be another soloist then, he'd play for the second soloist, but the celebrity one would still be sitting with us. No shine on them, no fuss with them at all. When they used to stay overnight, they didn't put them up in a hotel, they'd find somebody's house to put them up. But what these classical people, these celebrities, would say, as soon as Maelor Richards was playing, 'This man would make his fortune in London.' He was brilliant, one of the best they'd ever heard. We were always sorry that he ended up in Rhos and didn't go any further.

Mary Hughes, born 1924

Anne Ziegler

ANNE ZIEGLER — the Liverpool lyric soprano and "Nightingale of the B.B.C.—is one of the most versatile and charming singers today. She is equally at home giving a classic recital at Wigmore Hall, as playing principal boy in pantomime or as leading lady in big musical shows. Her broadcasts of the leading roles in "Love Needs a Waltz," "The Chocolate Soldier," "The Geisha" and "Princess Charming" and many other varied programmes, have established her reputation on the air as a singer with a beautifully clear crystal voice and a delightful personality. Miss Ziegler is, in private life, Mrs. Webster Booth, and she first met her husband when they played "Marguerite" and and "Faust" respectively in an all-colour film of Gounod's "Faust."

FOUR

A celebrity concert programme signed by Anne Ziegler and Webster Booth. (Mary Hughes)

RAC rally, 1967. (Kris Morrison)

Webster Booth

ONE of the most popular tenors of the day, Mr. Webster Booth makes a welcome return to the Cefn concert platform. Described as an operatic star who ranks with the finest in the world, he has appeared in the International Opera Season at Covent Garden, played leading roles at the Theatre Royal, Drury Lane, and the Savoy, has sung at the Albert Hall, Queen's Hall, and all the principal Provincial Concert Halls and has gained widespread fame on the wireless and as a gramophone recording artiste. A native of Birmingham, his remarkable talent has been acclaimed not only in Great Britain, but in the U.S.A., Canada, South Africa and the Continent, where he has toured with outstanding success.

FIVE

Photography

My father did some photography, for his own personal interest, I think, because when we left Plas Kynaston Terrace, we had the big white earthenware developing dishes, and he had a plate camera. He had the back bedroom for the darkroom and he used to have a big wooden shutter that he put up. He had an old bicycle lamp to make the red light.

Kathleen Smith, born 1923

RAC rally

The RAC rally used to come through Newbridge once a year. I used to go down to the bridge with my brother Wincenty, he was learning to take photos and develop them. At least one car would always go over the bridge, the turning was so sharp and the cars going so fast. They stopped the rally a few years later.

Kris Morrison, born 1952

You, you and you!

My father had an allotment and when the weather was right, he'd say, 'You, you and you!' or, 'Bill, I want you to come with me tonight and we're going in the allotment.' Digging and planting and all things like that. [We grew] everything. It kept the house going. The expense on the household wasn't so great. Peas, potatoes, beetroot, onions, lettuce, radish, all those kind of things. And of course we were engaged in something and that was life to us. If my father said, 'Let's go to the allotment', we were thrilled to death! It was a pleasure to us. A good life.

Bill Davies, born 1912

Dad's revenge

I remember Dad planting all sorts of vegetables and the boys picking them up, checking the roots and things, checking that they were growing and of course they all had to be replanted.

Then, before the crop was even ripe we used to pick them up and eat them and so there was nothing left when they were supposed to be ready. So that went by the wall. There he was – no money, no tobacco, no fags. So he decided to grow tobacco. We used to think that was lovely, they're lovely plants. We didn't know it was tobacco at first – just nice strong plants, nice little flowers. Then we had to pick all these leaves. 'What you picking those for, Dad? What are you hanging them from the ceiling for?' They were like bats hanging everywhere, drying out, from the ceilings, under the beds, everywhere. And then we had to put them with apple core and with rum, or with a bit of sherry, experimenting on the flavour. We used to say, 'What are you doing this for?' 'Smells nice, Dad.' Until he started to smoke it! And then it was, 'Is that Monsanto's?' 'Dad, have you taken your boots off?' 'No, it's Dad's tobacco!' 'You better run, it's Dad's revenge!'

Kris Morrison, born 1952

Pigsties

On the 1873 OS map there's nothing here; but the 1912 one, the houses are here, and these little things at the bottom of the gardens, these are pigsties because everyone had a pig. My Dad was into gardening in quite a big way and I can remember his first greenhouse was at the bottom of the garden and it was built using a brick structure that was already there and he said he could remember, as a little boy, coming to his grandparents and there being the pigsty down there.

Diane Powell, born 1946

Hanging the pig

My taid was very keen on the garden, so the garden was always full of fruit and vegetables and in the summer there was always things like peas to go and pinch. When we renovated in

'95, we found all sorts of things like the old inglenook fireplace, because there are photographs of it when it was with a kitchen range and you used to kill the pig and hang it in your living room.

Janet Williams, born 1965

Pet pigs

I always remember the things my Dad used to do to put food on the plate. We all had these pigs. Helena had one called Stumpy that used to lie there still as anything and we used to pretend it was dead and tell her it was dead and she used to bawl her eyes out. Michael had one called Spot. I remember him chasing it around the village with a mop because it had this big patch on its spots and he was trying to rub it off – he chased it all round Newbridge to try and get it off. But when it came to the first slaughter, Dad took it to Harrison's, which is now Tŷ Mawr and of course all the children cried out, 'We can't eat that, Dad, it's our pet! We can't eat those!' We wouldn't eat our pig – no way!

Kris Morrison, born 1952

Hunting

The otter hounds used to come by the river. The ladies would have green jackets and tweed skirts and a long stick, and the gentlemen would have a green jacket with a cap on and all these hounds and they would go along the river, on foot. And of course the hunt used to come around the park as well, the foxhounds, because the foxes would come to steal the chickens in the night.

Betty James, born 1922

Fishing for eels

My grandfather used to take me fishing, late at night when it was dark, down by the draw-

Janet Williams' grandmother and her pigs. (Janet Williams)

bridge, and he used to thread wool through the worms, so he had a bunch of worms attached with string to a stick. He'd drop the bunch of worms in the canal, he'd feel the eels go for it, and he'd flick the bunch out of the water. And, because there were no hooks, the eels just fell onto the path. I had the job of putting them in the sack and then sitting on the sack – which was moving, because the eels were still alive – and looking after them. The canal eels were never quite as good as the river eels.

Dennis Williams, born 1931

Tickling fish

I would never like the fish from the canal; they always tasted earthy to me. There used to be some nice fish in the brooks in Garth and we used to tickle the fish and we also fished in the reservoir and part of that was used for stocking fish for Whitworth's. The land was all owned by one landlord, Colonel Whitworth. He used to chase you off his land and we used to go after his fish, his fish stock in the reservoir.

Edward Jones, born 1937

Swimming

Most lads and girls used to love swimming. We used to swim in the reservoirs, in the canal, and it was quite deep. It was quite dangerous really because the canal had broken bottles in it and a lot of my friends were carted off to hospital because they would swim in the canal and then they'd walk along the bottom, and they'd suddenly lift their feet out of the water and there'd be a thick slice out of their toes.

Edward Jones, born 1937

Home-made swimming costumes

You couldn't possibly avoid the canal, living in Fron. You'd dash home from school on a hot summer's day and you wanted to go swimming, and your mother'd get a jersey, a boy's jersey, and cut the arms off, and that's where your legs went in, and then use a boy's tie, holding it up. So it was grand until you jumped in, and then as the wool got saturated with water, the home-made swimming costume became very heavy and used to pull you down, you know. Happy days. I'd say most of us learned to swim in the canal, under those conditions, jumping in the canal, in our best jerseys.

Dennis Williams, born 1931

Pigeon racing

I used to race pigeons in the Cefn Mawr Homing Society. It was quite a popular pastime in the early part of the twentieth century. Pigeon clocks haven't got fingers on, they have a dial, to tell the time. The dial used to rotate and when the pigeon was clocked, a needle used to puncture the dial, to record the time. It was quite involved. They used to send them by train, take them as far as 500 miles away, to France, let the pigeons off, time the journey, and it's worked out on yards per minute, the fastest pigeon covering the distance. That's how it's done. There were some very notable fanciers from Cefn. You can go into Wrexham Museum and there's records about all kinds of sports, but there's nothing on pigeon racing, yet it's probably one of the most popular working-class pastimes in the area.

Howard Paddock, born 1944

Billiards

I was working in the pit, the Wynnstay Colliery, and we got our money on a Saturday, and we couldn't do anything until Saturday afternoon. We'd come for a Saturday night; you couldn't move on a Saturday night. The main place I used to go was the Holly Bush, and across the road, there was a pub there, and we used to go there. The thing that stands out in my mind is one night we went there and the [billiard] balls jumped off the table and straight in the fire. That was the end of that; we didn't go there again.

Tom Evans, born 1909

Playing with a tin can

You were considered posh if you had a football. It's hard to believe now but sometimes we played football with a tin can because we didn't have a ball.

Edward Jones, born 1937

The Challenge Cup

Charles Butler was the honorary secretary for the Druids, it was his sons who were the footballers Windsor and William Butler. I've got the letter from Sir Watkin Williams asking Charles to set up a time to present the cup when they won the Welsh National and Border Counties Challenge Cup in 1879/80. William was in the Druids when they won the Challenge Cup in 1897/98.

Mary Hughes, born 1924

Cricket

John Archer was a brilliant amateur cricketer of his day. He allegedly hit the ball from the Bont playing fields right over the aqueduct! In the summer they played cricket there, Monsanto had a cricket team – they played their own fixtures there. John Archer was a member of the Monsanto cricket team.

Warren Coleman, born 1937

Right: *The Froncysyllte first eleven for the 1909/10 season, outside the Aqueduct Inn. Dennis Williams' grandfather is in the middle row, seated extreme right, wearing a suit. (Dennis Williams)*

Below: *Cefn Druids eleven 1879/80, winners of the Welsh National and Borders Counties Challenge. Charles Butler is in the back row, extreme right. (Mary Hughes)*

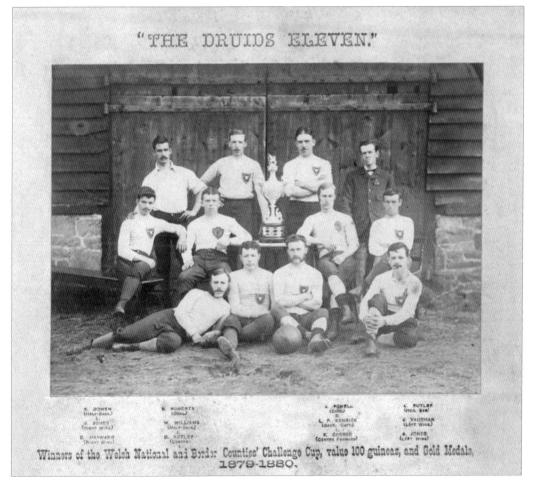

"THE DRUIDS ELEVEN."

F. BOWEN (HALF-BACK)   E. ROBERTS (GOAL)   J. POWELL (BACK)   C. BUTLER (HON. SEC)
J. JONES (RIGHT WING)   W. WILLIAMS (HALF-BACK)   R. P. KENRICK (BACK. CAPT.)   E. VAUGHAN (LEFT WING)
D. HAYWARD (RIGHT WING)   D. KETLEY (CENTRE)   K. GEORGE (CENTRE FORWARD)   J. JONES (LEFT WING)

Winners of the Welsh National and Border Counties' Challenge Cup, value 100 guineas, and Gold Medals, 1879-1880.

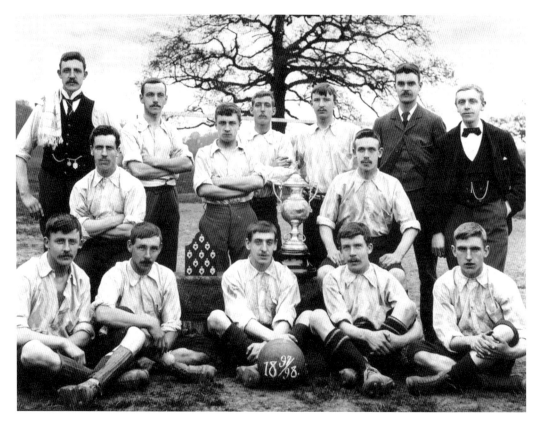

Cefn Druids, 1897/98. William Butler is in the middle row, extreme left. (Mary Hughes)

A terrific batsman

I had a cousin in Llangollen, Tom, he had a terrific bat with him, he hit the ball over the aqueduct, right out of the field, over the top it went. Tom Diggory, he's dead now but he could give it a wallop, he was a terrific batsman.

Cecil Diggory, born 1920

Monsanto cricket ground, at the foot of the Telford Aqueduct, 1960s. (Flexsys archive)

three

Work

The General Strike

In 1926 a General Strike took place through-out our country and my father, being a coal miner, was out of work for quite a long time. There was an enormous amount of distress and poverty at the time, as all the working men in the district – Cefn, Fron, Garth, Trevor, Acrefair, Chirk – were without employment, and support from the authorities was very meagre. There were some large pits and brickworks operating in the district in those days, employing several thousand men, and I think the strike lasted for six months. My memory of that time is going to the soup kitchen which had been set up in one of the outbuildings of the school – it may well have been very close to the schoolhouse. I'm not certain whether I went every day but I do remember going there on several occasions. It was a very hard time for my parents, with no money coming in to the home. Luckily I'd got one older brother only so we were a small family. However, you can imagine the impact it had on the large families of those times – six or eight children was quite a normal family and there were several families of that size in Fron, who must have been severely hit.

Emrys Roberts, born 1922

Sheep rustling

During the 1926 General Strike, I can remem-ber being marched at lunchtime to Hill Street Chapel to have a lunch because our fathers were out of work. Some children were taken to Morris's shop in Cefn and given a pair of boots because of the situation. They were hard times. We were so hungry that my father and his friend, they decided they'd have to go and steal a sheep from Sir Watkin's field, so they went at midnight and they caught a sheep, and neither of them had the heart to kill it, so we didn't have any mutton. They just let it go. But we survived.

Betty James, born 1922

The colliery

It was hard at the colliery. I had a job once, early on a Sunday night, to inspect the area. We went about eight o'clock. We went in a body there and when you go in gas like that, your lamp goes. It was very dangerous.

Tom Evans, born 1909

Carrying the wages

I often think of the security of children now. But then, you see, my father had about six men working for him. When he would go to fetch all the money which he paid out to the different ones, he would have to go back down the pit, but I would go to Ruabon to fetch the money for my mother to have in the front room and then they would come to fetch their wages. They all knew that I was going to fetch this, and yet there was nothing to think that there would be any danger, only that they would wave as you went and yet I was carrying this money, these wages for six men – you couldn't do that now. I'd be about ten then. I would sit in the engine house waiting for all this and that and different ones would come in – and it was payday wasn't it? I'd have a penny, two pennies. I was coming home quite rich!

Margaret Roberts, born 1919

Dick Iron Man's girl

My father and two of his brothers, they had the shield for North Wales for being the first coal cutters and they had the job of opening different faces in the Hafod. And the Hafod men would say, 'Whose daughter are you?' 'It's Dick Iron Man's girl.' My Dad was called Dick Iron Man, because the coal cutters that they were using to open up, they used to call them the iron men because of this machinery. So they called my Dad, he was only 5ft tall, the Iron Man. So of

THE WORKMEN'S COMPENSATION ACT, 1925.

Report of Medical Practitioner under Section 12 (3) of W.C.A., 1925.

IN THE MATTER OF THE COMPENSATION OF:

Name of Workman Harold Pennington.

Address of Workman Dolydd Road, Cefn Mawr, Nr. Wrexham.

Occupation Collier. Age 33

Employed by Black Park Colliery Co Ltd.

Date and Place of Accident 23rd August, 1944. Black Park Colliery.

Nature of Accident and how caused Miner's Nystagmus.

Nature of Injuries Miner's Nystagmus.

Present condition of Workman His visual acuity is not impaired, and his pulse rate is normal. No oscillations of the eyes can be detected.

Is man incapacitated from working? NO.

If so, is the incapacity total or partial?

Is incapacity due to the accident?

Grounds for the opinion of the Medical Practitioner. No signs of miner's nystagmus can now be elicited.

Signed Edward F. Wilson M.B.

Dated 4th day of January, 19 46.

An accident compensation form from a 1944 pit accident. (Janet Williams)

Plas Kynaston Colliery, now Saunders garage showrooms. (Arthur and Barbara Humphries)

The Butler family outside the bakery in Church Street, Rhosymedre. (Mary Hughes)

Charles Butler and his horse. (Mary Hughes)

course I went home and I said to him, 'Well, I never knew your name was Dick Iron Man!' 'Oh you've met some rogues!' he said to me.

Margaret Roberts, born 1919

Dust and heat

Gary: Black Park [Colliery], terrible hot place, that was. Dust was the problem with that job, it was enough to kill you. Silicosis it gave you, the miners' lung disease.

Peter: My taid lived here in Cefn and they'd walk to Black Park because there was no transport in those days. Then once they got to Black Park and went down the pit, they had to walk between one and two miles underground to get to the face.

Gary Roberts, born 1945, and Peter Wright, born 1936

Pie Shop

When the Green Pit, the Wynnstay Colliery, was open, I lived in Rhosymedre with my aunt. I would have been about fourteen, I suppose. She had a shop and used to bake the pies. Meat and potato pies, apple pies and everything, and the men used to come off afternoons [shifts] at ten o'clock, and the wives would come and they'd say, 'Will you make me two meat pies, or whatever you have, by ten o'clock, by the time the men come home?' They'd cook the potatoes, and my aunt would have all the pies and the gravy ready for them. I think it was four pennies for a pie, and then the men used to call to the Wynnstay pub and have a pint on the slate.

Gertrude Jones, born 1915

The bakery

My great-grandfather, Charles Butler, he was a baker. Butler's was the baker and Nichols' was the butcher. My Great-Uncle William Butler took over the bakery and he kept it with his spinster sister, Annie. They used to do public baking there, particularly at Christmas; everyone took turkeys as well as their cakes and bread. You never saw Uncle Will unless he was covered with flour from head to foot. I was told by Annie Butler that she used to watch him making oven bottom loaves – a big round bit with a small round bit on top and you stick your finger down the middle – well, he used to do that with his elbow!

Mary Hughes, born 1924

At the café

I used to work in Llangollen, years ago, when there was a café on the canal. I was working there with this lady, and I remember I was there one day, making tea and that, and I said, 'I like this man's voice.' So she told this fellow. 'Oh, thank you,' he said. And it was Gwyn Williams: he's a fellow that was singing and all that, years ago. Well, he was chuffed.

Maggie Saunders, born 1915

Order lad

I used to be an order lad, with a big bike with two big baskets on, because people didn't have cars in those days. So they'd come in, put the order in and we'd put the order up, and I'd deliver it. I'd be doing that from four to seven, Thursday and Friday, and all day Saturday, while I was still at school. I got fifteen shillings for that, for the three days. I wouldn't have done the job if it wasn't for the tips, but I used to make a pound in tips, roughly, and at Christmas I'd make five pound in tips. The only thing that kept the old shops going, you got free delivery. If you lived in the top of Cefn, it was a benefit to have it all hauled home for you.

Pete Garrett, born 1949

Butcher's boy

My father used to, as a boy, deliver meat for the local butcher, Jack, who had the Co-op butcher's in Froncysyllte. He had all the meat in his basket on the front of his pushbike and he used to have to pedal back and to delivering the meat to Cefn and Trevor and places. One day he fell off his bike into the canal with all the meat for the delivery for the Sunday lunch that day. He had to rescue the meat and he knocked on the door of an old lady that used to live near the canal and she said, 'Oh, don't upset yourself, I'll sort you out.' So she washed it all under the tap, wrapped it in newspaper for him and put it back in the basket for him to deliver for the Sunday lunch, or it would have been his job on the line in those days if the butcher had found out. And for weeks afterwards, people were going into the butcher's saying, 'I can't understand why our meat came wrapped in newspaper this weekend for lunch,' and the butcher said, 'Do you know anything about it?' and my Dad just shook his head and claimed he knew nothing about the situation. He found out though – and he made my Dad scrub every inch of the butcher's from top to bottom! My dad's sixty-five, so it's about fifty years ago. His name's Raymond Jones.

Karen Wright, born 1965

Raymond Jones with his cousin, c. 1952. (Karen Wright)

The post

After the war, I came and worked in the post office, delivering mail. I delivered to Cefn, Rhosymedre, Acrefair, Lancaster Terrace, the Plas Madoc estate. It was hard work, believe me. And at Christmas time we'd be there half past five, I used to get up half past four every morning to go to the post. We were there all day, Christmas time. We used to have a great big furniture van bringing it. It was cold in the cellar there and damp underneath, and we've come out and the snow's been up to my chin, me being little! And we were all on foot. It was hard work, all hills. We only got paid till half past nine and we were there til half past ten, eleven sometimes, and we were going back by two. Two pounds something I had, when I first started. And [it was] dark, very dark. I had to have glasses sooner than my time, because you're looking [at addresses] in the streetlight, the lamplight. Many a clout we had, slipping and falling. The dogs, we used to have them all following us. I had one, up in the top of Cefn. He used to sit on a wall, waiting for me, by the grocer's shop, and his name was Rebel. And he'd sit on that wall, every day of the week, but he would not sit there on a Sunday. He knew! He'd wait for me. I had to go over the bridge, over the railway line. He wouldn't come over the railway line, no, he'd go back, but he'd be waiting for me, next morning. And they moved to Wrexham. And you know, that poor dog, he was on the wall, and his poor feet were raw, and he'd walked all the way from Wrexham to come back to me. Somebody took him home. Everybody knows me. It doesn't matter who you speak to, they say, 'Oh, I know who you want, Gertie the Post.' That's how they know me. Still now.

Gertrude Jones, born 1915

Hairdressing

[I had a shop] in Cefn. My sister had it first. The war came, so my father wouldn't allow me to go away to be trained. My sister was trained, so I worked with her. I grew up into it and I carried on with it after I was married. Mind you, it was very different from what it is today. The dearest [style], that was a Eugene, and if you undertook to do the Eugene perm, you had to agree to charge a guinea for it, which was a lot of money in those days. The other one was the Wella. But the prices we charged were stupid. If I'd only charged what we should have done, I'd have been well off today. I don't think I was intended to be rich!

Kathleen Smith, born 1923

Hughes and Lancaster's

I started work when I was eighteen years of age and I worked in the time office of Hughes and Lancaster's, which was an engineering works which eventually became the Butterley Company and is now Air Products. Time office is like a wages department, [working out] how many hours they've done in a week. During the war, some men were called up and women

Hughes and Lancaster's reunion, 1991. (Betty Thompson)

went and worked on the machines, which they hadn't done before. Of course, when hostilities ceased, the girls finished because the fellers were coming back to resume their duties. I stayed on there; I worked there until 1971. I worked for the three firms: Hughes and Lancaster's, Butterley's, and Air Products.

Betty Thompson, born 1922

'All Their Yesterdays', from the works magazine of Air Products, 1991

Fifteen girls, aged between 66 and 77, from Leeds, Holyhead, the Isle of Wight and local villages, got together during the summer to recall the time, fifty years ago, when they all worked together at Hughes and Lancaster's, now Air Products, Acrefair.

These were the girls who were drafted into war work in an industry they knew nothing about. However, they soon learned to operate capstan lathes, fine limit grinders, drilling and key-seater machines, as well as carrying out some fitting work.

They brought with them memories of twelve-hour shifts in one week, one week days, and one week nights, making parts for tank turrets, although they were never actually certain that this is what the parts were. They weren't told anything as, in those days, careless talk cost lives.

Five of the group married men they worked with, and were only allowed three days for a honeymoon. Their nostalgic evening was very enjoyable, remembering their bosses, and their foremen: Bill Evans, known as 'Bill Thou' – thousandth part of an inch, you see – who always wanted 'another thou off, please' when they were machining, because they were working to very fine measurements; another Bill Evans, who was known as 'Hurry up!' because he constantly urged every one to do just that; and Mr Robertson, a dour Scotsman, whose lack of height nicknamed him 'Little man'.

The girls would like to thank Air Products, whose gift of dinner wine was greatly appreciated and thoroughly enjoyed.

Betty Thompson, born 1922

Picking tatties

[I remember] picking tatties at Peregrine Hall, when we were in school, one and six a day.

Gary Roberts, born 1945

A shilling a week

A shilling a week was [earned from] running with the milkman. He had the big churn and you would take the jugs from the people.

Margaret Roberts, born 1919

Working for the milkman

When I left school, I went to work for a milkman in Gobowen. I slept in there, on the job like. So I was doing that for a couple of years.

Bill Davies, born 1912

Land Army girl

I was asked, would I go to a farm in Denbigh? They wanted somebody for cows and somebody for field work. So I went on the cows.

The Land Army badge. (Gladys Peters)

Gladys Peters (left) and Jean from Manchester hoeing between tree seedlings on the Pulford estate, Gresford. (Gladys Peters)

It was smashing. There were 100 cows, milk cows, and every afternoon I used to bring all the cows up, with a bull. I'd have run a mile, years ago, I wouldn't have gone near a field with a cow, never mind a bull, and I used to bring 100 cows, every afternoon, on my own. But I was told, the bull won't take any notice of you, you're just shouting the cows, 'Home, we're home!' The cows were washed twice a day, all their behinds and their udders and their legs, and the tails were shampooed once a week. It was a great place to work. All you had to do, with washing and milking and going around with all the milking machines, and when they were all finished with the milking machines, you had to go around with your bucket, to take the last drops. Sometimes you didn't get all the milk out of the cows, they'd hold the milk, and then when you'd come to them, perhaps you'd get so much more out of them, and that's what you had to do every day. It was a wonderful life.

Some places you went to, soon as you got there, 'Come on girls, your breakfast is ready!' There'd be bacon and egg, fried bread, sausage and things like that. About half past ten to eleven, you'd have sandwiches and cups of tea; come dinner time you'd have a great big spread, the table would be just loaded with food. About three o'clock, they came out with sandwiches and cake, cups of tea. When you finished at five o'clock: 'Come on girls, before you go home!' and they had a lady there that was doing all the cooking and she was making bread, home-made bread. You know the great big vessels they had, the round ones, the very old-fashioned ones, of clay? She'd have a great big round one, holding it in her arms, cutting bread, and we used to have bread and jam and cups of tea before going home. It was a marvellous farm, and then you'd get half a crown when you finished. It was wonderful!

One job I did like was going out threshing. And more often than not, I got on the box, cutting bands. When they were cutting the sheaves, they're strung with the machine. As they drop out, they're taken to the base and built up. And then when you come to threshing, they're taking up sheaves, chucking them onto the box. I'd be cutting like mad, chucking them over, it was great! And the seeds were coming out the other end. It was all bagged to make your flour and everything else, wheat, oats and barley, whatever they had growing, in the green crop.

Gladys Peters, born 1921

Plough horses

The old ploughing horses, they were something special, seeing the farmers getting the threshing machines taken around, to beat the corn, and get the flour. They'd have six horses pulling them, because of the hills, and it was quite a sight. In the summer, you wouldn't be asked, you'd just go and help the farmers, and everything was with a pikel, putting the hay onto carts pulled by a horse. The ploughing horses were called Boxer and Flower. They were beautiful things. They were so big and powerful, and yet they seemed to have lovely natures.

Dennis Williams, born 1931

Coachman

The Hughes side of my family came from Cerrigydrudion, they became anglicised when they came down here, working for Graesser. But he was a good employer. It started with my great-grandfather bringing a horse down here from Cerrigydrudion, for someone in this area. Then he looked for a job and he had a job with Mr Graesser, as his coachman. I know Mr Graesser wasn't amused when the horse used to pull up at the coachman's favourite pubs. Well trained! But he kept his job.

Dennis Williams, born 1931

Lord Howard Dewallden's stables

I went to work for Lord Howard Dewallden, Chirk Castle, in the stables. I used to be there for eight and finish at five, that was the hours. But when you're working with animals there's no hours. I didn't study the hours while I was there, early or late, working late I wouldn't mind at all. I loved the job. I didn't care how hard the work was, I loved it. We had forty brood mares and four stallions, and we bred every year. At foaling time, I was there nearly all the while. The ones that were born this year, well next year they'd be two, then they'd go to three and we'd break them in to riding, hunting and we broke them in to harness. We had the big coach, the four-in-hand, with the Dalmatian dog underneath. If the daughter phoned down to the stable to say she wanted to take it out, well we'd have to get it all ready and she'd have it out. And when she came back, oh, a lot of work, a terrible lot of work. I was there for twelve years. I left there to go to the Army. I left to go in 1940 and I had five years in the Army.

Bill Davies, born 1912

Such poverty

My mother's mother had a shop on Queen's Street. There was such poverty. People would say they'd pay at the weekend and they wouldn't be able to. She had to give up in the end.

Diane Parry, born 1944

Rations finished it

[My father] Wilfrid was a shopkeeper, he kept a grocer's shop. The shop went downhill during the war. Rations finished it off. When I was a kid, during the war, things would come and the boxes had been opened and all the stuff pinched out of them. And then the Co-op came and ruined my Dad. Co-op

W.F. Humphries builders outside Maelor House, 1950s. His yard was at the back of the Eagles. Wilfrid Butler is standing in the first row, fourth from right. (Mary Hughes)

customers would come after hours, 'I've run out of tea', and like a fool he'd give it to them. He went to work for W.F. Humphries afterwards.

Mary Hughes, born 1924

The Co-op

I worked for thirty years for the Co-operative Society. It was a thriving society. Where the Wheatsheaf workshops are now, the offices were. Vans went round all the areas. I was doing work connected with the shops. I used to do a job called 'shorts and overs', working out what they'd had in, what had changed in price, that kind of thing, a leakage system it was, and I used to deal with debts, I had to go to the County Court for the debts, and I didn't like that very much.

Rhona Roberts, born 1928

A Co-operative Society commemorative mug from 1926. (Kathleen Smith)

Journalism

My father was a journalist. He used to be in the old Wynnstay Colliery and then, the year I was born, he went into journalism. He used to send copy to the *Daily Post* and various nationals and then it went on from there. Our phone number was Ruabon 65 and I can remember the telephone, the candlestick type, a tall one. He used to put copy over to the *Daily Post*, 'Liverpool Central 48400' and then, 'Moss, Ruabon, copy.' And then he would dictate and the girl in Liverpool would copy it down on a typewriter as he dictated. And he would give her Welsh words. Well, to Liverpool it was foreign, wasn't it? 'L for London, N for Norman, E for Eric, M for Mother' and he would get his copy across like that. He used to report the local news, anything going on in Monsanto, any fires. I can remember one time there was one and he sent a report in to the *Daily Mail*. My Dad sent a straightforward report and then in Manchester they must have dressed it up a bit, and referred to 'firemen clinging perilously to ladders'. Monsanto took a dim view of that, because it sounded terribly dangerous.

Kathleen Smith, born 1923

In service in Liverpool

My grandparents were both in service in Liverpool and they met in the Welsh Baptist Chapel in Prince's Park, and they came back here because the First World War had started and my dad was a toddler, and they didn't want to be in Liverpool. But then my grandad went to work in Monsanto, which I think must have been horrific for someone who was used to working outside.

Diane Powell, born 1946

Courting in Manchester

My nain went into service, she was sent to Manchester once she was old enough. She worked in a big house in Manchester. She met my taid then, because they used to tell me stories about him coming on the train to visit her when they were courting. Then when they got married they came back and they went to live in Temple Vale, which is the row of red-brick terrace houses near the Queen's and that was actually across the road from the house where I live now, from the house which used to belong to my great-grandad. There's quite a bit of land with the house, there's about an acre and half out the back. They used to keep pigs and chickens and a couple of sheep. My Mum was born in the '30s and at the time all the women were working in Monsanto, which would have been a munitions factory then. So my mother was brought up really by my great-grandmother.

Janet Williams, born 1965

Quality control at Monsanto

In the Analytical Building at Monsanto we were testing and quality controlling finished products like pharmaceuticals and rubber, e.g. aspirin, phenol – paracetamol was just starting production run in the 1950s.

Edward Jones, born 1937

Health and safety

Safety and clean working environment then, as now, had a high priority in [Monsanto] chemical works. To improve and encourage this, safety and cleanliness competitions were run – the winning lab or workshop had a winner's draw. The analytical building has been demolished, and the site is now clear.

Edward Jones, born 1937

Never had a cold

I worked in Monsanto. I did twenty-seven years in Monsanto. The last plant I went

The north frontage of Monsanto's Ruabon Laboratories. (Edward Jones)

Michael Henderson (then of Abbott Street, Wrexham) during a Sunday dinnertime break in the top laboratory of the Analytical Building, Monsanto, c. 1960. He is seated on the marble slab where specimens were weighed for assay and analysis. (Edward Jones)

Works manager Mr K.H. Handy presents David Ledgeard of Cefnybedd near Wrexham with a Parker 51 pen set won in the Analytical Department's winner's draw. (Edward Jones)

in, and the first one as well, actually, was the aspirin plant, and I've never had a cold! I don't know if it got in my system, funny, isn't it?

Bill Davies, born 1912

J.C. Edwards

Between Tower Hill and the Duke of Wellington, there are two cottages. Well, they were the original offices of J.C. Edwards. Then they moved to offices on top of the hill in 1900. I was eighteen when I started there in 1940. I was there twenty-three years. I started on fifteen shillings a week on a three month trial. Then they gave me a pound a week. I started off as a wages clerk. The feller that was doing the work said he'd give them a fortnight to get someone, because he was going to volunteer for the Navy. My friend was working at J.C.'s, so she told them I wanted the job, so I went for an interview and got the job. But what happened? He didn't go! He just didn't go, so I was sort of surplus. So they put me in the other office, shorthand, typing, but I didn't like that, I liked working with figures. Things did work out. He walked out one morning, he didn't say he was going, but he took his cards. And then someone else walked out, I expect he'd been called up. I replaced three people that had gone. They gave me a rise to one pound ten shillings. I was in J.C.'s all the war, and I stayed with them till they came and said they would be closing the works in 1963.

They didn't have carbon paper before the war or during the war. They had big books and blue linen cloths which they soaked in water. The letter to be copied was put in the book with the wet cloth and then placed under the press, a terrific press. Then when it'd taken the copy you would take the letter out and they'd have a big ornamental fire with a grill on the top and you used to dry the letters on the grill. Well you can imagine what they looked like, but that's how they sent them out, all crinkly. That's how it was done till they had carbon paper. We used to cook toast on the gas fire for our lunch.

There were two sections in the Trefynant works. They used to make the salt glaze pipes in one and adamantine and glazed tiles in the other – the encaustic section. The clay for the tiles was brought from Pen-y-bont, which was their other works, the other side of the river, in Newbridge as you go to Chirk. In Pen-y-bont, they had a big clay hole. There used to be four mills, one for each seam of clay. You'd have the rough soil and stones on the top. Then you'd have a layer of clay, for the common bricks. Then you'd have another layer of clay which would be for the quarry tiles. Then another

Aspirin packing shed at Graesser-Monsanto Chemical Works Ltd, c. 1924. (Flexsys archive)

layer for the terracotta and the bottom layer was called 48, which was ground into dust for the adamantine tiles, pressed and made in Trefynant. The adamantine tiles were fired in the beehive kilns, then the ones to be glazed in various colours would be dipped in glaze, placed in a sagger [a clay trough] and refired. They made the tiles for the *Titanic*, made fireplaces, wonderful big pipes and salt glazed sewer pipes.

Lydia Jones, born 1922

The head office at J.C. Edwards. (Lydia Jones)

The directors' room at J.C. Edwards. (Lydia Jones)

J.C. Edwards salt glaze pipes. (Lydia Jones)

J.C. Edwards Trefynant works (Lydia Jones)

J.C. Edwards Penybont clay hole crusher No. 2. (Lydia Jones)

Choosing a grate

I was about seven and we went to J.C. Edwards, tile makers and grate makers, and we went to choose a grate. You would choose what tiles you wanted and then go to choose a design. I remember it well and there were lots of different designs you could choose. But everybody did that. They were very fond of cream and green, with a fawny colour going through. You could always tell a J.C. Edwards grate: cream background, then the arches around green and fawn. I think they cost about £20, in the early '50s.

Diane Parry, born 1944

Unintentionally ornamental

J.C. Edwards had a wall at the Trefynant. It was made of the faulty bricks they had made, seconds. It wasn't intended to be ornamental, it was just a practical border, they just stuck anything in, but it was really interesting. They used to do pipes, so there'd be engineering bricks and all sorts.

Mary Hughes, born 1924

Friendly brick

I was digging in my garden one day and I found a brick. I picked it up and I saw it had writing on so I traced it with my finger: J…O…E…Joe? What sort of name's that for a brick?! I washed it off under the tap and then I saw, of course, it wasn't Joe at all, it was J.C.E. But I still kept it, by the taps in my kitchen.

Gwyneth Feathers, born 1939

Mean old man

I know somebody who worked there [at J.C. Edwards] and he was very mean, wasn't he, the old man Lloyd? [Lloyd Edwards was the owner of J.C. Edwards.] She went into the works and she was working there and he said, 'Will you go to Cefn to get the prescription for me?' And of course she walked to Cefn and she walked up to the Oreb, to Bryn Ogar which is up the hill, and she knocked the door and said, 'Here's your prescription, Mr Edwards.' 'Oh thank you very much, wait a minute, wait a minute' and he put his hand in his pocket and gave her a polo mint!

Iola Roberts, born 1933

Shed of song

Work places, people used to sing, you see … at J.C. Edwards in the Adelph, they called it, in the pot room, they had a big long shed. They made the big chimneypots and vases and all fancy stuff. All the men that worked in that pot room were preachers and lay preachers. Every Sunday, one'd be going to one preacher, another would be going to another chapel. And on a Monday that shed would be full of song. They'd sing all the hymns on the Monday that they'd been singing on the Sunday.

Gary Roberts, born 1945

four

Wartime

Can you remember?

I can remember, when I went to school way back, always on Armistice Day we were taken to the war memorial, this is for the First World War. But children now, they've no idea.

Olwen Wright, born 1920

Hitler in Cefn!

The day that war was declared, I remember, opposite Air Products was the Drill Hall and it used to have 'Drill Hall' in the bricks. And the TA branch of this area used to meet there and go out onto the football field and drill, you know, military drill. And the day that war broke out, an armed guard was posted outside the Drill Hall door. An armed guard! I thought Hitler was in Cefn. Frightened me to death!

Betty Thompson, born 1922

We can't find your auntie

I was on holiday when war broke out. I had a message from my uncle, Jack Share Jones, to say, 'We can't find your auntie. She's on the Continent, she's in the Mediterranean, on a liner, and she might have to go to America, the long way round.' And he said, 'Can you come? I might be having forty blind evacuees this afternoon.' Sid Bowen worked for the RDC [Rural District Council] and they sent him to fetch me, and I was in Cefn, in the school, taking children and their sandwiches, taking them to addresses. I had a list of addresses – Mrs So-and-so was having two. Evacuees. They'd come off a train, from Liverpool.

Gwyneth Partington, born 1919

Arriving with gas masks

The Acrefair evacuees, we all met in Trinity Institute, and they arrived with their gas masks,

Cefn war memorial before it was moved to its present location. (Arthur and Barbara Humphries)

dragging along the floor; some had paper carriers, some had little cases. It was sad.

Marjorie Tod, born 1920

Gas masks

We used to go with the gas masks, used to have to have gas masks. You went into school. School was the main object for everything. You had to go there and learn how to use them; then you'd have them at home. We'd go after school or at weekends. A gentleman came in to show us. It was a bit frightening, they were horrible-looking things.

Audrey Owens, born 1938

Evacuees in Fron

To be fair, in Fron most of the evacuees weren't necessarily complete strangers. They came from Liverpool or London but their grandparents were there, or their aunt or something.

Betty Jones, born 1938

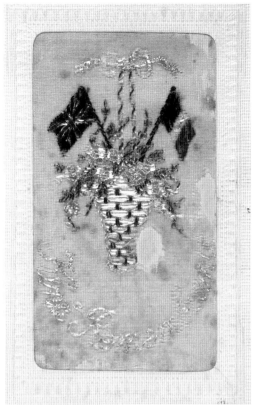

A postcard sent from France during the First World War. (Janet Williams)

Phil Blake

All the evacuees were coming, from Liverpool and from London. I made friends with one of the evacuees from London, Phil Blake. He married my sister. Phil stayed in Fron with his mother and two sisters. He went back after the war but then my sister and Phil took a fancy to each other and that was it. But all these evacuees came. All that was compressed into possibly the first twelve months of the war, because then everything changed. Hitler had other things to think about. The bombing intensity stopped and a lot of the Liverpool evacuees went back home, more than the London lot. I think all the terror side of it was in the early years, after that it got a little bit more fun, I suppose.

Dennis Williams, born 1931

Johnny Bananas

Johnny Bananas was staying with us, in the war. He would be about twelve, thirteen. He was with my grandparents but he was a handful: he was a real city slicker, from Liverpool. They couldn't handle him. Well, he had an air gun and he shot my mate in the bum. I know Vince's mother could have killed him! He was too much of a handful so he went back.

Dennis Williams, born 1931

The air-raid siren

When the war came, well, nobody had shelters here. In fact the first time the siren went, the next morning everybody said, 'What was that about?' It was like a ship's siren and nobody knew what it was for. They found out after, of course, it was the air-raid siren. We didn't realise the danger we were in, I suppose. Uncle Fred next door, he was in the First World War. It had gone a bit quiet one night and he went outside. He heard – I don't know whether it was a bomb or the aircraft – and he went flat on the floor, on the yard, because he'd been in the First World War, so he had some idea.

Kathleen Smith, born 1923

Under the cinema steps
Nobody'd got air-raid shelters in the early part, so Mr John Owen Jones allowed my father and Uncle Fred to put forms [under the cinema steps]. So we used that as our air-raid shelter in the very beginning. You'd got the steps coming behind you, so you went under, so you'd got the overhead cover, and we used to sit there till the all-clear went.

Kathleen Smith, born 1923

In the cellar of the Eagles
I can remember air-raid sirens going. We lived then in a stone house in Church Street and under the stairs there was quite a big space. We used to go under the stairs when the air-raid siren went. I've also been in the cellar of the Eagles pub, Rhosymedre. The licensee used to let people go in the cellars until the all-clear sounded.

Rhona Roberts, born 1928

Only a nightie
We hid under the stairs, we were pushed right down, and my dad was going out on this ARP thing, or fire thing. I can remember my mother grabbed this mac from behind the door to put on herself. When the all-clear

Wilfrid Butler in his Acrefair Fire Service uniform. (Mary Hughes)

came we came out and put the light on and we were in stitches. My mother had only got this shoulder and that shoulder, out of the back of the mac she'd made a gas mask cover, all the back had gone, there was only a nightie there!

Mary Hughes, born 1924

Looking for Monsanto's
I can remember something coming down quite near here [Tŷ Mawr], down by the river, a plane or something. The planes used to come over, they were looking for Monsanto's. My father was working in Monsanto's. He was in the ARP. He used to go off on training and my mother never knew where he'd gone off to and how long it'd be before he came home.

Betty Jones, born 1938

Plane crash
What I do remember, during the war, is a plane which crashed just over the park wall, near where the Park View nursing home is now. Right over the wall. The pilot was killed.

Rhona Roberts, born 1928

Bombing raids

When the war came, there were no lights at all, pitch black. When the moon came out, it was absolutely brilliant because there were no lights anywhere. In Wynnstay Park they had searchlights and anti-aircraft guns. If they found an aircraft, all the searchlights would move across the sky to shine on the trapped aircraft. It looked beautiful but I never heard a gun fire. The sky was black with waves of German bombers coming straight over here, to Liverpool.

Dennis Williams, born 1931

Those are the Germans

The first time we heard aircraft, in our innocence we thought they were ours, till my brother, who was at Dunkirk, came home on leave and he heard them, and he said, 'Oh no, those are Germans.' There was a certain throb to the engines, you see, a different sound, I suppose. They used to come over here to Liverpool, and at one stage they had to drop their bombs on Garth. It set the gorse afire and it burnt for quite a while. Some people said a farmer had shone a light but we understood they jettisoned the bombs. And you've probably heard of Lord Haw-Haw, and people said that he referred to it, because they came back and they did drop one or two bombs on it.

Kathleen Smith, born 1923

Guarding Garth Mountain

They didn't bomb this mountain for very long. The first bomb was dropped and it set the gorse on fire and they thought they'd got something there and they bombed it the following night

The wartime fire service during the time of the bombing of Garth Mountain. Wilfrid Butler is in the middle row, third from right. (Mary Hughes)

and the following night, for three nights, I think. One of the chaps in Dad's choir, he worked in the office in Monsanto, he was sent to guard Garth Mountain. He was petrified! He was there all by himself and what he was guarding nobody knew. He had to stay there all night on top of the mountain. Apparently he was grey by the morning, he was so terrified!

Mary Hughes, born 1924

Convoys

We'd have all the convoys coming down here from Holyhead, coming down the A5, the Americans, with big trucks pulling guns. It was amazing. Sometimes a convoy pulled up along this top road, and they'd stop for the night. My grandfather said to me: 'Go and ask a couple of the soldiers if they'd like to come for a bit of supper, and something to drink.' I remember going down and I walked along, and these trucks are so high, you know, and it was like: 'Hello, anybody like to come?' And two soldiers came; they were Geordies. I brought them up to my grandfather's, he was giving them a drink of whisky; my grandmother was giving them something to eat. Then back down into the truck, and then they'd be off. That was that.

Dennis Williams, born 1931

Collecting souvenirs

I used to like to chase aircraft that had been shot down, or come down for some reason, to get souvenirs. You could make nice things out of the perspex from the windscreen; it wasn't glass, you could work on it. One came down in Rhosymedre. Well, I was on my bike there quick, before the police. One came down in Pentre, one on the castle, Dinas Bran, but that was in such a mess it frightened me, so I came from there quick, in case I saw something I didn't want to see. One night, we were stand-

Roger Williams (left) and his American GI friend Charlie, 1943. (Dennis Williams)

ing in the village and around the corner from Llangollen came an air transporter. On the back they had a German Heinkel bomber and they went into the Brit for a pint. We were up on this Heinkel bomber with our knives, having a wonderful time, getting the souvenirs. If you could get the German cross, which was the aircraft identification, you were lucky. You could easily cut a plane, it wasn't metal, it was only canvas.

I was sitting here one day and I saw a barrage balloon, with the cable hanging from it, drifting quietly up the valley. I got on my bike and it came down just above the golf club. And I was there first. I had great big pieces of it and all the lads were cutting it, and the next few days in Fron, all the mothers had these lovely big bags, made from barrage balloon material, for shopping bags.

Dennis Williams, born 1931

Guarding the aqueduct

Did you know that the aqueduct was guarded by the Home Guard? They guarded it with shovels and brushes. They hadn't got any guns. I don't know what they were going to do – sweep them off the bridge or what!

Diane Parry, born 1944

Dad's Army

The village Home Guards were just like *Dad's Army*; it was hilarious really. Their captain, Joe Jones, wasn't a soldier but a solicitor's clerk. He was a grand chap. They had a sergeant, Harold Gough, who was a real soldier, from the First World War, so he knew what he was doing. They'd be down on the Recreation Ground in Fron with broomsticks and all funny things and I remember when we were up this tree and we were pelting them with twigs and things. We had no respect.

Dennis Williams, born 1931

Dancing with Americans

I wasn't here in the war, I was in Birmingham. I was nursing there, you see. There was an American camp right by us; we used to go to the dances with the Americans. All the big things in Birmingham, they used to ask us to go. Course we didn't have much during the war, did we, but we had plenty because of the boys, you see. They had marvellous parties, really good times. It was hard working when we were looking after them but after, you know, we used to have great times. See our boys hadn't got it but the Americans had got everything, they used to give us chocolates, we came back loaded. The only time we got anything off our boys was NAAFI night. They used to give us things then: chocolate, cigarettes and different things you couldn't get during the war.

Eluned Griffiths, born 1924

May 1943. The Denbighshire/Flintshire Home Guard Bn. marching through the streets of Acrefair. Many Ruabon employees served in the local Home Guard during the war.

The Denbighshire/Flintshire Home Guard battalion march through the streets of Acrefair, 1943. (Flexsys archive)

Roger Williams' official Royal Army Medical Corps photograph from around 1942. (Dennis Williams)

American on a horse

Before I was married, I got friendly with an American soldier. Lots of girls went to Wrexham and met the American soldiers. They were in Penley. He was wounded in the war. He thought he'd come across to my place. But he had a horse from somewhere! Somebody told me that there was an American on a horse. He'd taken the wrong turning, he didn't come up to Acrefair, he went on to Rhosymedre and he asked somebody walking in Rhosymedre, 'Can you tell me where Miss Butler lives? She lives in a shop.' I lived in a shop as well. They took him to my Auntie Annie. She was old and she had her hair combed down and pulled back so it looked like she'd got a snood on. She always fluttered her eyes for some reason, she had a funny habit of it. She was really, well, prim. She worked hard. So this soldier was looking for me and they took him to her – same name and lived in a shop. Poor Auntie Annie, she'd have had fits, this American soldier walking in the door!

He'd come over from D-Day – he was in D-Day. He was shot through the shoulder and he was at Penley. My Dad's choir was entertaining in Penley, you see, so as you do, you walk up to everybody's bed, don't you, and talk to them, soldiers away from home. We went two or three times, and when he got on his feet afterwards, he said, 'Well, I'll come across and talk to you.' That's as far as it went; he went back. He was very smart, a very nice chap, used to write to one another, but there's no future in that is there? It was a wartime thing.

Mary Hughes, born 1924

Chocolate and black pudding

During the war, everything was rationed: food, clothes. We didn't feel it as children but my mother was worried. I think, with my father being in the Army, we had extra help with clothes. There was certainly help and we had free meals in school. And my grandmother was very good with me because she gave me her sweet coupons. I remember when chocolate first came back; it was like paradise! It seemed to disappear and then it came back quietly. You'd go with your coupons – beautiful! It was a big day when bananas and oranges came back. We kept a pig, in Tŷ Uchaf; everybody kept a pig. A pigsty went with the house. And the pig was our pet, so we had to clear off when it was killed because we were all getting too upset. But once it came back, we enjoyed it. Black pudding! We had a wonderful time.

Dennis Williams, born 1931

Queue in the butcher's

I remember saying, if war came, it would be quite funny having to stand queuing for food. It was very different, our stocks were going down, we couldn't get food and we were rationed and mother was ill. I used to get up in the morning and go and stand in the queue in the butcher's before I went to work. Then the little red van, Griffiths the butcher, from Ruabon, would go in by the little Co-op shop on the corner and he'd have sausage. Someone said, 'Go on, I'll keep your place, run, get sausage!' So I would and then I'd go back to the butcher's.

Lydia Jones, born 1922

The judgement of Solomon

Everybody had ration books for food and ration coupons for clothes. In the Co-op shop you'd put your ration book into a box, so you would have your turn. Some people used to try to go out of turn but this system stopped it. The rationing didn't end until 1953; the last thing on ration was sweets. At one time even bread was rationed. Cakes were short, that kind of thing. I remember one time, two people wanted the same cake. To settle the issue, the shop manager cut the cake in two, to satisfy his customers.

Rhona Roberts, born 1928

Never seen a banana

There's nothing like a first-hand account, is there? You can read it in a book but when you hear it as it really was, I mean, the talk about the depredations of the Second World War, well, I was born in '37 so I was very young during the war but I can still remember wondering why, in the books I read, they had plenty of fruit and everything. I'd never even seen a banana or a grape.

Edward Jones, born 1937

Arrowroot and white of egg

I mean, maybe I was wrong, but I did it because of family. Anything going black market, I'd pay. I remember we had a dog and the poor old dog was ill – we took him to the vet, he had distemper or something like that. And the vet said, 'Well, what would your mother give him?' I said, 'Arrowroot and the white of egg'. 'Well if you can get that, give it to the dog.' I'd got some eggs for ten shillings … my wages were £1 at that time, so that was a lot of money, wasn't it? My father used to go 'Bloomin' egg!' He would have the yolk, but the dog would have the white. It worked, though, for the dog, we had him for six or seven years after that.

Lydia Jones, born 1922

Women's Voluntary Service

When the war came, I was a hairdresser so my father looked into it and I was allowed to stay at home because they felt that the munitions workers needed their hair done, it was for morale. So I was allowed to stay at home but I had to join the WVS and we used to go to Plas Kynaston, making camouflage nets, you know, putting the strips on.

Kathleen Smith, born 1923

Nursing in Birmingham

You could either go into the forces or the factories or nursing or something like that. So I decided to go into nursing, you see. So I went to Birmingham and when I got there, there was this military hospital and my friend and I went there. They used to bring all the casualties, all in uniform. We had to undress them and look at their wounds. We used to hear the bombers coming over, the planes running heavy because of the bombs, and then we used to hear them going back lighter, when they'd dropped all their bombs.

Eluned Griffiths, born 1924

Bulbs painted blue

We were [at J.C. Edwards] during the war. Course we had blackouts. The bulbs were all painted blue and you just had a little circle there about the size of, used to be a florin then, you know, a 10p. And that's where we were working, underneath that, and blackouts at the window. I've got, at home now, a little piece of red crayon. You couldn't get things in the war, so when you wanted a red pencil, they'd only give you a half one. You used to cut a piece off the end and put your name on it to show for a replacement.

Lydia Jones, born 1922

The Land Army

I was asked to go to work on a farm; the girl who was working there was going on a week's holiday. 'They'll give you a fortnight' – and I stayed there two and a half years. It was grand.

Gladys Peters, born 1921

Driving for Monsanto

When I married and there was the war, I went down to Monsanto and I was the only woman holding a licence at that time, so either I would be sent away – as I was what they called mobile, with no family – or I could take the job of driving, so I went to go on to the big Scammells. It's a three-ton unit and you have three big trucks, one with a big cover, the others were flat and they're articulated. I was working the three big trucks with two other men there. I was only six stone two then, and there were no self starters or anything on them and you had limited petrol then. You started it with a handle. And then, there weren't the nice roads, there were only tracks, weren't there? So when I started first there was a wager on that I wouldn't do it, you see, with some of the others and I was determined that I would do it! But in the meantime, Johnny, he was from Llangollen, he took me on to learn. We had to unlock every gate then, because of sabotage or anything, so you had to keep getting in and out with the gates. I can always remember – I wasn't used to the big wagons behind me and I was very short – so I more or less had to lean straight out. We came to the laundry gates and I leant out, and the next thing, we took the gates with us! Poor Johnny. 'Oh Margaret!' he said, 'We will never do this!' But I did! And the main gates, we had to keep blowing for the gatesmen to come out. Well, I found that if one gate was open I'd get the unit through. But you know what happened, I came up with a truck and forgot, didn't I, so I took that other side gate off as well! I wasn't flavour of the month at the time.

Margaret Roberts, born 1919

Marchwiel

In the war, I worked in the Royal Ordnance Factory at Marchwiel. We'd go to Wrexham on the train and then they'd transfer us to buses. And some were open-top buses, that they'd had from London and places like that. We'd go to the factory and it was quite a big place – it was three miles – through the factory. The units were mostly underground and you were searched, you weren't allowed to take any matches or cigarettes, tobacco or anything inside the factory. You would go into your department, change your clothes for special clothes that they had: white top and trousers and you would have a pair of shoes, with rope soles, and you would take these shoes with you, and when you got to the unit, you would have to change your shoes. You weren't allowed to walk on the floors with any grit on your feet in case you caused a spark. Before you went out from the dressing room, you would be searched again, to make sure you hadn't got anything on you that was contraband. It was quite dangerous. We were packing cordite.

Betty James, born 1922

The entrance to the Monsanto works after the Second World War. (Flexsys archive)

Pitch black

I worked on ammunitions during the 1939 war, in Marchwiel. Underground we were, working with cordite, and the cordite used to smell terrible. We had to get on a train, get on a bus from Marchwiel, from the factory, and come to Wrexham station, and if the troops were going, moving at night, we had to wait until all the troop trains went. Pitch black, everywhere black. We all used to cling together, going down and coming back.

Gertrude Jones, born 1915

Buckingham Palace

My husband was in the Army then. We were married in 1942, when he came home on leave. My two brothers were in the Army and an aunt of mine, she was in the Army. She was a matron. She went to Palestine in 1938. She was a reserve with the Queen Alexandra's Imperial Nursing Service and then she went from Palestine right through Iraq, she went to India. She didn't come home until 1945. She was awarded the Royal Red Cross Medal, First Class, and went to Buckingham Palace to be decorated by King George VI.

Betty James, born 1922

Monte Cassino Cross

My Dad's name was Wladyslaw Jurkojc. He was born in what is now Belarus and first he fought the Russians, then he fought the Germans. He was wounded twice. The first time he was fighting the Russians, around 1937, he was in a scout jeep and was shot through the knees. He was taken to a Polish hospital under German occupation and the German surgeons did a great job on his knees. He was later caught by the Russians and sentenced to fifteen years in Siberia as a German spy. When the Second World War broke out, he was released to fight the Germans. In Monte Cassino he was leading six lorries of ammunition to the

Wladyslaw Jurkojc, dressed as a Cossack for the Cefn Carnival, 1967. (Kris Morrison)

front at night when his motorcycle ran over an artillery shell. He was blown off his motorbike and one of the lorries he was leading ran over him. He was awarded the Monte Cassino Cross. After eleven months in hospital in Italy, he was on the Red Cross ship coming over to England. He was on it five days and he heard on the way that the war was over. He arrived in Liverpool on 15 May 1945 at 3.00 p.m. and it was raining.

Kris Morrison, born 1952

Thousand-bomber raid

My knees, I've got no knee caps, no patellas is what you call them, isn't it? I haven't got any, I got smashed up, you see. I've got a stiff leg in one and only half a bend in the other. But what I say is, I was very, very fortunate. But the most exciting thing for me in the Army was when they had the thousand-bomber raid on Caen. You couldn't see no sky for planes. I don't know whether you remember them saying they were going to have a thousand-bomber raid on Caen, but it was the first one they had and the sky was black. You'd never believe it if you saw it. We were on a hill above Caen, and, oh, what a sight, but a terrible thing, wasn't it. A slaughter. Just slaughter it was – for everybody and everything. I don't hold with war at all. So it's a good job we haven't had one for quite a while!

Bill Davies, born 1912

The fallen

There was a lad along here, he was good-looking, he was a lovely lad, Wynn Roberts, and he came straight from Dinas Bran School into the Air Force. He came home on leave and the next thing, he had been shot down and killed… The lad who sat beside me in the choir, John Parks, his dad was blown up in a tank in Libya or somewhere. It was going on all the time. In the village, they had a shop window and they put all the pictures of the dead there. I remember standing with John Parks there, and him saying, 'There's my Dad there' and wishing, just for a moment, 'I wish my Dad was there with all these heroes!'

Dennis Williams, born 1931

War memorial

I think there were five lads from the village that were killed. They are on the war memorial in Cefn and they've got a memorial in church at Rhosymedre.

Betty James, born 1922

Party in the Stute

I don't remember much, but I remember when the war finished. They gave all the children a party in the Stute [the Church Institute]. The Stute's not there now, they've got a

Above: *Land Girls marching at Buckingham Palace. Queen Elizabeth stands on the podium with a basket of Denbighshire produce beside her. (Gladys Peters)*

Right: *The book of remembrance from the unveiling and dedication of the war memorial in 1926. (Kathleen Smith)*

community hall in Fron, but right by the side of the canal house was what we called the Stute. Then they took us all to by the drawbridge and somebody brought a radio out and there was the end of the war speech from Churchill. All the children from Fron – and there were evacuees there as well.

Betty Jones, born 1938

Parties on the road

When the war finished, we had all these street parties, wonderful, wasn't it! All these parties on the road. They even took us one day up the mountain.

Audrey Owens, born 1938

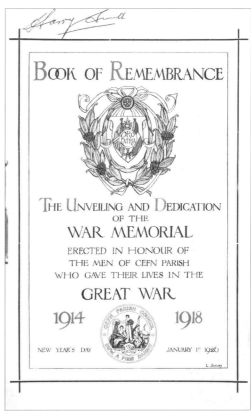

BOOK OF REMEMBRANCE

PRO
PATRIA

THE UNVEILING AND DEDICATION
OF THE
WAR MEMORIAL
ERECTED IN HONOUR OF
THE MEN OF CEFN PARISH
WHO GAVE THEIR LIVES IN THE

GREAT WAR
1914   1918

NEW YEAR'S DAY   JANUARY 1st 1926

Heroes of the First World War from Froncysyllte. Edward and Bob Hughes were Dennis Williams' mother's uncles. (Dennis Williams)

Froncysyllte war memorial. (Emrys Roberts)

Organising a street party

It only took a couple of days, everyone was cooking themselves. People would come out with balloons and everything, everyone would rally round. It wasn't down on the main street, it was up by the school and then further along where we lived. Tables would be put out and things. Of course, there wasn't the traffic then.

Audrey Owens, born 1938

Billets for the Eisteddfod

I tell you what we did look forward to. Fron was the first place after Llangollen to take foreign visitors for the Llangollen Eisteddfod. In the first years there were no dancers, but the first year they had dancers they came to Fron to see if we could billet them. Well, the first years of the Eisteddfod it was still coupons, rationing, so the first thing they did was issue all the competitors that came with ration coupons. Of course they gave them a month's worth of coupons, they were only there for a few days and most of them didn't want them anyway! So we all had an extra month of coupons and sweets! At that time you could put a hundred up in Fron. And at that time, some of the houses hadn't even got bathrooms. And as for putting two men together – you wouldn't think twice! You'd say I've got a spare bed, I can take two, I'd rather have women, or I'd rather have men, or a married couple, they slept together, that was it – you wouldn't dream of it today!

Betty Jones, born 1938

five

Singing, Sundays and Celebrations

The Land Army farewell parade

In 1950, it was the final parade, in London, for the Land Girls and I was chosen to represent Gresford hostel. We all went together on the Friday morning by train from Gresford to London. On the Friday afternoon, we went to Waterloo Barracks and the soldiers were there. We were in our rows and we had to march like all these soldiers did, in a straight line. They kept telling us, 'If only you could see yourselves!' We had to keep doing it over and over again, until they thought we were in straight lines. On the Saturday, we went to Buckingham Palace, 500 of us. Queen Elizabeth, not the one that's Queen now, the late Queen Mother. She was dressed all in mauve, with fur. She spoke to every fourth girl. And she stood straight in front of me, and I thought, 'Ooh, she's going to speak to me' and she turned slightly ... and she spoke to the girl next to me, and she was from Flintshire. Oh, and I was mad! But it was a lovely experience. It was absolutely marvellous. We felt so proud to be there.

Gladys Peters, born 1921

Coming together in song

The Llangollen International Eisteddfod started in 1947 and ... the boys were coming home, after the war, in Froncysyllte and they thought it would be a good idea if they formed a choir and they'd have something to get the village together as the boys came home.

Betty Jones, born 1938

The choir

The choir has played quite a big part in my life because I joined it when it started. The leader of the youth club, Wilfrid Jones, was quite a keen singer and when it was announced that they were going to form a choir, he took us all along. Could have been about fourteen or sixteen of us. We went along and I had a look – I couldn't believe it, all these old men sitting there – well, I thought they were old men, anyway. I don't know how we stuck it but we went to choir practice. I suppose there wasn't an awful lot to do in those days, apart from the pictures and things. And then we had our first little concert and we called in a pub. Some of

Nave

ST. PAUL'S CATHEDRAL

NATIONAL
HARVEST THANKSGIVING SERVICE

Saturday, 21st October, 1950 at 4 p.m.

Ticket Holders are requested to be seated by 3.45 p.m.

W. R. MATTHEWS, Dean

A ticket for a National Harvest Thanksgiving Service at St Paul's Cathedral. (Gladys Peters)

Queen Elizabeth talks to Land Girls at the farewell parade at Buckingham Palace, 1950. (Gladys Peters)

The first appearance of Froncysyllte Male Voice Choir at the Llangollen International Eisteddfod, 1948. (Dennis Williams)

the blokes in the choir bought us a pint. We thought, 'Hey!' Here we were, under age, but here they were, treating us well, you know, so we thought, 'It's not so bad, now.'

Dennis Williams, born 1931

Cor Meibion Froncysyllte

I suppose the choir has become such a famous choir really because of Llangollen. We went to Llangollen, straight away, to compete, and we must have been dreadful. Lloyd, our first conductor, had tremendous patience. He knew what he wanted; he was dragging us quietly up to their standard. I remember hearing the Moravian Teachers' Choir; they were fabulous. They were in a big semicircle and I remember thinking, 'If we can ever sing like that, it'd be great!' Well, we got there, we certainly did. We crept up there, quietly.

Dennis Williams, born 1931

Disasters and triumphs

We went to Glyndyfrdwy, singing in that little village hall. The lighting came from a generator and, in the middle of our concert, the generator broke down so we were all in the darkness. But we somehow muddled along until the generator came back on. In fact, we were singing in the George Edwards Hall and a water pipe burst above us, and the first bass were showered with water. We were in a chapel in Gwersyllt and we could hear strange noises and these noises were getting louder and louder until the bottom bass quietly sunk. The staging was collapsing underneath them!

We went to London to sing and that was fantastic. There were no motorways then, it was down the A5 all the way, with Bryn Melyn buses from Llangollen. That was very exciting. We sang in Westminster Central Hall. It was a competition and the test piece was 'Martyrs of the Arena', which is a real good piece. I felt like a martyr too because I was in the front. I was a first tenor. One of our first tenors fainted and he was in the second row, so they all held him up until we finished the piece. I always remember him, John Ernest Davis his name was, but for some reason they always called him Tiddler. Well, they took him out and they had him underneath a tap and as he was coming round, instead of being sympathetic, some of these old men were playing hell with him, 'What did you do that for?' I thought, 'Well that's a bit hard, he couldn't help it.'

Dennis Williams, born 1931

Wilfred Butler's choir

There were different choirs in the area. As well as a male voice, there was a very good mixed choir in the Cefn, Wilfrid Butler's choir. That was in the '50s. I used to come across from Fron to Wilfred Butler's choir.

Betty Jones, born 1938

Cefn Mixed Choir

As a young man, my Dad [Wilfrid Butler], he stammered. This is the tale he used to tell us: he stammered and he was told that it was breath control, so his mother sent him for singing lessons. He went to singing teachers and started to sing and found that he could control it quite well; the breath control for the singing helped the stammer. Not many people knew that he had a stammer, it was only when he used to get a bit excited about something you'd hear it slightly, but I didn't even know that he stammered from the time I was born. He was a tenor soloist. He must have joined the Cefn Mixed Choir. Emlyn Davies, the conductor of that choir, was a music tutor in Bangor, very nice fellow, Welsh Baptist he was. He must have seen that he could do it and when Emlyn retired, Dad took over.

Mary Hughes, born 1924

Froncysyllte Male Voice Choir, Chirk Castle, 2003. (Dennis Williams)

Cefn Mixed Choir, 1933, with Emlyn Davies, conductor, and Wilfrid Butler, sub-conductor. (Mary Hughes)

Cefn Mixed Choir in the 1950s. Conductor Wilfrid Butler is front right; accompanist Mary Hughes is in the middle row, extreme right; and Diane Parry is in the middle row, fourth from right. (Mary Hughes)

Cefn Male Voice Choir

The British Legion had a small group and the fellow who ran it wanted somebody else to take over and my Dad took it over from that and it was recreated as Cefn Male Voice Choir. They gave him a presentation plaque in 1944 to celebrate ten years of the choir. I never ever heard him sing publicly: he'd finished with the singing, he was more interested in the conducting. He loved it. And then he had the other choirs, you see: Weston Rhyn Choir, Chirk Choir, what we called the naughty boys' choir – Quinta, it was! It was a home for delinquent boys and this fellow wanted help with it, so Dad went to help him with the Quinta Choir, and there was the youth choir ... dear me, he was out nearly every night!

Mary Hughes, born 1924

Accompanying the choir

I started with this choir when I was fifteen, then of course I went to college and then Dorothy played and probably when I had the children someone had to play and I packed in eventually. I played the organ in Seion Chapel – how many years? Fifty years?

Mary Hughes, born 1924

Sing it again

We were chapel, Methodist chapel, all our lives. My father was rather a good singer and ... we'd have a hymn and if there was a chorus in the hymn, he'd always sing it again, always. And it's funny, I never thought anything, but I started the same. If there's a hymn and it's a real good one and there's a chorus, I'm off again. In the chapel, they got used to it, knew what was coming like! Well, we were on holiday in Rhyl and we went to the Methodist there and they had a bloomin' good hymn there and of course when we got to the chorus, well naturally I opened up again, didn't I? Everybody

was stunned, you see. So after I give them the first line, they could see what was happening and they all joined in, didn't they? After the service, the preacher came to me and he said, 'Mr Davies, I remember that from years back. It's a shame it's been stopped'. How it stopped I don't know, but they hadn't had it for quite a long, long while. So it took them all by surprise, but the minister loved it. You sing the chorus after every verse and then when you got to the last verse you'd sing the chorus and then again. Beautiful. It would bring me to life, you know, I used to get a beautiful feeling. [My favourite hymn], oh, there's so many! 'How Great Thou Art', 'Praise Be', I can't say I have a favourite because they're all my favourite!

Bill Davies, born 1912

Three times on Sunday

We went to church three times on a Sunday: in the morning; Sunday school in the afternoon and nighttime. It was very serious. We weren't necessarily all Welsh-speaking, so one of the things we did was to teach them Welsh. But we did Bible stories, lots of singing and concerts. We had good teaching though. It was the last time that they were at school. They were leaving day school at fifteen but sometimes there would be a young people's class at Sunday school.

Betty Jones, born 1938

The Welsh Jordan

When it was fine, the Reverend E.K. Jones used to baptise at the Bont, in the river. We were talking about it, with my friend, and we said, 'Remember E.K? He used to baptise them in the river.' Because John the Baptist, he baptised Jesus in the river. I was baptised in the chapel up there.

Gertrude Jones, born 1915

Cefn Male Voice Choir outside Plas Kynaston. Wilfred Butler flanked by Dorothy Jones on the left and Mary Butler (later Hughes) on the right. (Mary Hughes)

The Baptist church in Froncysyllte. (Betty Jones)

A baptism performed by Revd John Williams in the early 1920s. John Williams came to Froncysyllte in 1920 and left in 1925. (Betty Jones)

Three trees

We had a minister in our chapel then, I was a big Baptist, I was baptised in the chapel, in the well. We had a gentleman, a minister, who used to take us up to three trees on top of the mountains to pick winberries and then we'd have a picnic on the top there. He used to take us once a month for a service. And I remember him taking us up there when the war finished.

Audrey Owens, born 1938

Sunday school anniversary

We used to have Sunday school anniversary for the first two Sundays in June. We'd look forward to these. We'd practise recitations and songs beforehand, for weeks. Then we'd be all rigged out in new dresses and straw hats, with patent shoes, and the boys would have grey flannel trousers – but they'd be short, because they didn't wear long trousers till they were fourteen – and a white shirt, with a striped tie and a snake's head belt to match, round the shorts. For the first Sunday we would all gather, at a quarter to ten, and the Salvation Army band would be coming playing; they were going to lead us around the village. And so we would go off, and every now and then we would stop and sing a song, and then the afternoon service would be packed, and the evening, with people coming to hear the anniversary. We'd be sitting on the stage, big ones at the top, coming down to the small ones at the bottom. As your name was called, you stood up and did your piece. They would invite someone to preside over the anniversary, and they would look for someone who was a bit well off, so that they could give a good donation for the Sunday school. Of course, everyone wore a hat in those days, and the ladies would come in their straw hats trimmed with flowers and veiling, and the windows on the sides of the pews would be full of the bowler hats belonging to the men.

Betty James, born 1922

Sunday school treat

I was belonging to the chapel, in Seion, Baptist chapel, and you had to go to Sunday school. Now we never had buses for trips, we used to go beside the aqueduct. We used to have a bun and a penny and a bottle of milk, that was our Sunday school treat, and then after, when the chapel got a bit better off, we used to have a charabanc, to go off to Rhyl, to Sunday school trip.

Gertrude Jones, born 1915

Fish and trips

We used to go to Rhyl for the Sunday school trip. We'd have two busfuls! You had to take your own food, but my father always said, 'When we go for a day out, we go for fish and chips.' So we never had to take food with us. That was always a treat. When we went to the seaside, it was fish and chips.

Audrey Owens, born 1938

A special train

It was the only day in the year that most children would leave the village. During the year we would have a card, and you could put a penny a week on the card, or whatever you could afford, and this would be drawn out for pocket money. The Saturday would come, and we'd have a special train, and the platform would be crowded with parents and children, and we'd go off to Rhyl. Mostly Rhyl, sometimes New Brighton. When we got to Rhyl, all the children would have a large sugar bun and a little bottle of milk. Mr Edwards the beehive, in Rhosymedre, was a baker, and he would have been up early in the morning, to make these buns, because he wanted to make sure that every child had something to eat before they went off for the day. We would go on the sands, and paddle in the sea. My father always used to have a day off from the

Reverend John Williams preaches under the oak tree near Trevor, at the end of the bridge at Bont, early 1920s. (Betty Jones)

Seion Chapel Sunday school with minister William Owens, Mary Hughes' maternal grandfather, 1929. (Mary Hughes)

brickworks to come with us. After we'd been on the sands, we would go to the Cosy Corner for fish and chips, then call into Woolworths to spend what pocket money we had. Then go on the bikes: they were trikes, you know, that went round a circuit. I think it was sixpence for half an hour, or something like that. Then we would go to the Marine Lake, for the fair. Then we would come home. We'd be home about half past eight.

Betty James, born 1922

Trucks on the train

Our friends over the wall, we'd shout, 'We're going picnicking!' in the holidays. We'd go down to Acrefair station. We'd have our little carts with all our things in. We'd all get in the guard's van and up to Berwyn. They'd be eight or nine of us. There were five of them over the wall and I used to hang out the bedroom window and we'd shout, 'Where we going today? Get the trucks, we're going to Berwyn.' The trucks were boxes with little wheels, we'd put the little kettle and things all in and then we'd all come to the bottom of the road and get on the guard's van, up to Berwyn. We'd get off and we'd walk up to the mountains by Valle Crucis abbey. And we'd have our little kettles and stoves, the children would be all playing and we'd watch for the time to run back down and get the train. They'd really enjoy it.

Margaret Roberts, born 1919

Train to Barmouth

In the summer you could go on the train for something like one and six, you and your bike could go from Ruabon to Barmouth for the day, that was half fare of course. The trip on the railway line was really nice; once you'd got beyond Trevor, it was all countryside.

Pete Garrett, born 1949

The Terriers go to camp

At the side of the Drill Hall was the resident sergeant's house and it was called the Drill Hall House. There was always a sergeant and his family there, and he was in charge of the TA detachment in Acrefair. [One] day, 'Ooo, the Terriers are going to camp!' They used to go to Kinmel Bay. A big army lorry would come to collect them. All with their gear and their puttees on, and their uniform. Well, dear me, we thought they were going to China!

Betty Thompson, born 1922

Royal Welch Fusiliers

The TA detachment here belonged to the Royal Welch Fusiliers, you see, headquarters in Wrexham. Every year there would be a church parade, they called it, when the Royal Welch Fusilier Band and different detachments of the Royal Welch Fusiliers would all assemble at the Drill Hall, plus the TA that belonged. They would march in military fashion with the band leading and the regimental goat, snow white he'd be with gilded horns and harness and a long coat like silk. They would proceed from the Drill Hall, right through Cefn, service in the church and then process back. Well, as children we didn't go to the church because in those days if you said Rhosymedre, well, it seemed like miles. But as children we used to sit on the bank near the Drill Hall and see all this activity of the assembly. Then the big command came, the band struck up and you shuddered! And off they went. Well of course we had to wait for them to come back. Well they'd got to process from Cefn to Rhosymedre, have an hour's service and process back. So you can imagine our long wait. Oh, we'd take number plates, the registration number of the cars, which were few and far between, to while away the time. And then you would hear the band, strains of

B.R. 4452

British Transport Commission (W)   **EXCESS FARE TICKET**

ISSUED AT **LLANGOLLEN**   **G/81335**

Train _2·20p_ Date _16 Jan 65_

(month in words)

Ticket held No		Description	
From		To	
EXCESSED FROM	_Corwen?_		
TO	_Llangollen?_		
VIA			
(For alternative routes see book of routes)			

Cause and description of Excess	Class	No. of Passengers (in words)		Amount		
		Single	Return	£	s.	d.
Without tickets Description :—						
_SC...?_			_ONE_		1	6
Short of destination						
Out of date						
Difference between						
Second to First						

Valid until _One Class_ Collected by _____

Issued subject to the Regulations and Conditions in the Commission's Publications and Notices applicable to British Railways.

NOT TRANSFERABLE

Right: *A train ticket for the last day the train line was open, 16 January 1965. (Pete Garrett)*

Below: *Royal Welch Fusiliers, 1922. (Karen Wright)*

the band, underneath Acrefair bridge, which no longer exists, and straight up the main road. Wonderful Sunday morning.

Betty Thompson, born 1922

A new dress

We had fêtes every year, we used to have it down in Argoed Hall then, all the floats and everybody dressed up. I always remember then, my daughter, she came home and she said, 'Mrs Thomas has said that we've got to change our dresses' and of course, you were on very small money then. My husband always worked but never had big money. I said, 'Well, I don't know whether we can afford it, what was wrong with the dress you had last year?' Anyway, we did it, got it out, sewed it up so she wasn't any different from the others. We had a fête right the way along the village that would be, and then right down towards the Rec, by the drawbridge. She was an attend-ant with the queen. One child in school was picked for the queen and my daughter was an attendant and of course every year they had a different queen and different dresses, that was the trouble, wasn't it? But we enjoyed it, that was the thing, and we got there.

Audrey Owens, born 1938

The Rose Queen

I was the Rose Queen in 1933, when I was ten, and we used to process all around and go to the fields by the church, where there were stalls and rides of a sort and ice cream and all that sort of thing, and that was where the crowning ceremony took place. Well, my mother thought that a Rose Queen, it should be a rose colour. So, I was in tea rose yellow, which isn't a deep yellow, I'll say lemon, and I had a long velvet dress, and I had a green train, green velvet train lined with satin and edged with, like, ermine and I had a gold crown

The Rose Queen, 1933. (Betty Thompson)

and I had white shoes, which had to be dyed lemon to match the dress. I went in a landau, my dear, a horse-drawn landau, with two little attendants, and then the maids of honour came on decorated floats. You were the Rose Queen for the year and the following year you did the procession again and there was another queen crowned, and you were the retiring queen.

Betty Thompson, born 1922

Party for the Queen

We all got together on the bank for the Coronation and we made a big party, games and everything. We bought all the children the blue commemorative book and it had one of the medallions on, we collected all together and then Mrs Bates made the cake, a big

A Coronation party. Diane Powell, aged seven, is seated near the front, wearing a Union Jack dress. (Diane Powell)

crown. It was lovely weather. We were all on the banks over there. It was a real good time ... all of them together, all the lovely children. And I still, now, have the children of their children coming round.

Margaret Roberts, born 1919

Mum was the Maharishi

We always used to be in the Cefn Carnival every year. Everyone would borrow a lorry or a flat bed truck from somewhere. The floats started off at Monsanto warehouses and ended up in the Druid's fields; in later years they finished at Tŷ Mawr. In 1967 the Beatles kept going off to India to see the Maharishi and we had a theme of 'Make love not war'. We had Saunders' the coal merchant's lorry and my Mum was the Maharishi.

Kris Morrison, born 1952

Easter Sunday frolics

Cefn United and United Valley football teams used to organise charity events on Easter Sunday in aid of local charities, a bed push or a pram race. They always ended up at the Queen's or the Black Lion, or sometimes both!

Kris Morrison, born 1952

Seasonal celebrations

Highlights in the school year were the Christmas parties and the sports days held on Tŷ Isa fields. On the canalside at Fron stood the Church Institute, the Stute – the building is still there and I think at the present time it is occupied by a local builder. Its original purpose was for holding Sunday school and social activities connected with the village church, although the building was owned by

Above: *Kris Morrison (front right) and her mother (centre) on a Saunders' lorry decorated for the Cefn Carnival, 1967. (Kris Morrison)*

Left: *An Easter Sunday charity event in the 1970s or '80s. Wincenty Jurkojc, Kris' brother, is in the centre. (Kris Morrison)*

the Canal Company. Because there was no community centre at Fron at the time, the Institute became the place where all kinds of village functions were held, especially when it was equipped with a kitchen and toilet facilities. It was there that we had our Christmas parties for the school and the Sunday school.

Emrys Roberts, born 1922

Wonderful sings

We had wonderful sings in the chapel, we had plays. Even when my children were small we thought it was wonderful to have plays at Christmas and nativities and things like that. We used to go round singing carols at Christmastime, and what was that day?... Hallowe'en. We used to go round dressing up for that, dressed up as witches and that. We always had treats, everybody had bags of sweets by their doors, didn't they, waiting for you. [Even in the war] they saved them up.

Audrey Owens, born 1938

Carol singing

[The church choir] used to go just before Christmas and sing carols to the Graesser family at Argoed Hall, twenty or thirty of us, and they would treat us to a Christmas dinner in the Stute afterwards.

Emrys Roberts, born 1922

Christmas stockings

For Christmas, we were happy, eight of us, hanging a stocking up. They'd have nuts, an orange, sweets, everything like that to fill the stocking. When you woke up Christmas morning, you woke up very, very early ... and we'd all be there with our stocking, looking at what I had and what the others had, we were so happy!

Bill Davies, born 1912

Some crayons or a book

At Christmastime all we had in our stockings was an apple and an orange, some nuts, sweets. The big thing was some crayons or a book.

Edna Roberts, born 1936

St David's church choir outing from Froncysyllte in the early 1930s. Emrys Roberts is seated in the front row, extreme right. (Emrys Roberts)

First-footing

We had to wait for the man from Ruabon on New Year's Eve. He would come on his bike. My Dad was determined he would be the first in the house after midnight because he had black hair! We'd give him a gift, some money and a glass of wine. I used to feel sorry for him cycling all that way so late.

Mary Hughes, born 1924

New Year's Eve

We used to have some fun on New Year's Eve. J.C.'s had the hooter from the old Wynnstay Colliery. So Monsanto used to blow their hooter and we'd blow ours and see who'd go on the longest, we'd have these two going. And the fellow blowing J.C.'s wouldn't give in, oh no! He'd get the steam up that night!

Lydia Jones, born 1922

A Christmas postcard from 1906. (David Russell Roberts)

A Cefn Bychan New Year card, sent on 28 February 1905. (David Russell Roberts)

six

The Aqueduct

Over the water

I lived in the village of Ruabon ... and we used to come to Cefn for the pictures. There was a girl I met and it was the first time I'd heard this: I asked where did she come from, and she said, 'I come from over the water.' I thought she'd come from abroad! But she'd come from Fron. And they said in Fron, 'over the water' didn't they!

Margaret Roberts, born 1919

Don't look down

I worked on that job in Fron, on that widening improvement, when they widened the road from the church in Fron to the weighing machine by the lime kiln, I worked on that. I used to ride across on my bike in the morning. I had to be there an hour before the other men, to get steam up, see, and I used to ride across [the aqueduct]. I can walk across it now but I have to look in front of me, I have to look at the wireless mast and if no one comes to meet me I'm all right. I mustn't look down, you see. If I look down I get the jitters, you know.

Gary Roberts, born 1945

Too far down

A lot of my early memories are being taken for walks by my taid. He loved the countryside so he used to take me for lots of walks down the river and round the Plas-y-pentre farmhouse, show me where the old railway line was and where the canals were. When I was a teenager, living in Knutsford, coming here for my holidays, when I used to bring my friends, I always used to take them and see if they could walk over the aqueduct

The aqueduct, 1910. (Arthur and Barbara Humphries)

because it was so high up and everybody'd be like, 'Oh I don't want to go there, it's too far down!'

Janet Williams, born 1965

Came back in the car

Once I ever went across [the aqueduct] – not again. I took fright halfway and there was no other way but to keep going on. I came back in the car. The height is terrific, isn't it, but wonderful. Wonderful view.

Margaret Roberts, born 1919

Pulling the plug

When they started on the renovation work, I was chairman of the council then and I had to pull the plug. They said to me, 'You've got to come across.' I said to them, 'How far have I got to go?' 'Right to the middle to pull the plug.' I pulled the plug in the very middle. And then the water all came down like a waterfall. It's a huge thing. All of these men had to pull it and I just pulled it at the end. You really had to pull it. The men who were doing it had got it all ready. I didn't know. They'd asked me to come and then they told me, 'Oh, you're pulling the plug!'

Iola Roberts, born 1933

Renovating the aqueduct

They were replacing the bolts and painting it, rustproofing it. It must be about five years ago, they did the same thing, just emptied it and cleaned it up. I think they did it about every ten years. I missed it when they actually pulled the plug, I'd like to have seen it.

Neil Hayward-Fraser, born 1967

The aqueduct seen from upstream, during renovation work, with scaffolding visible. (Neil Hayward-Fraser)

Crossing the aqueduct, 26 November 2005. (Ed Fisher)

Conquering the fear

I used to work on the boat, taking tourists across the aqueduct, and if it was windy you'd get stuck in the middle of the aqueduct. The boat would be blown up against the towpath and the boat wouldn't go one way or the other. It was a bit of a laugh. I used to have nightmares about the aqueduct as a child. I used to dream I was running across it and then it would break and I'd be scrambling to get to the other side. And as soon as I went to work on the bridge it conquered the fear and I never had the dream again, but it was a recurring dream as a child. I was four when I first went across it, got taken over with Johnstown School. We were only small, we were all holding hands, we were all in the middle of the aqueduct and we had thunder and lightning, so maybe that's where my dream originated from. We were on the middle when the thunder and lightning started. We all got soaked and legged it back to meet up with the bus. An old gentleman on the main road allowed us all to shelter in his garage until the bus arrived.

Karen Wright, born 1965

Basin in a cloth

I remember, when I was young, going across the aqueduct with a basin in a cloth to take dinner for my great-uncle that was a widower. I used to go all the way from Well Street, cross the akkie, straight – but I couldn't find him, he'd be having a pint in the Brit, then I'd come back, have no time to have my own dinner myself and go back to school.

Gertrude Jones, born 1915

Paper aeroplanes

Bill Evans and I used to go by train to school, from Trevor. When we'd come home, we'd get to the centre of the aqueduct and we'd be making paper aeroplanes with our spare sheets of exercise books, and see whose could go the furthest. And it was amazing, if you got the wind just nice, they'd go for miles, down the valley. We really used to enjoy that.

Dennis Williams, born 1931

The river frozen over, c. 1950. (Dennis Williams)

Through the railings

My mother always used to tell us this story. When she went to the grammar school in Llangollen, you used to have to pay then. There were still horse-drawn boats on the canal at that time, in the 1920s, and there weren't buses to go to Llangollen like we had, they had to go to Trevor and catch the train. So if they started over the aqueduct and a horse was coming, they either went back and missed the train and were late for school or they went through the railings, through the gaps and stood on the other side until the horse went past and then got back on the path. And there was one boy and he couldn't be bothered to stand waiting, he'd carry on walking on the other side! It was mad what they would do to catch the train on time.

Betty Jones, born 1938

Walking on water

The Central [School] hadn't long opened and I really enjoyed it there. That's how we came to go over the aqueduct, but we never thought nothing of it ... rain, snow, ice – well, we used to walk on the water then. And we used to walk on the other side of the railings – anything for a dare. Then sometimes, if we met up with the lads, we'd go round the road, round the Bont as we called it, but it was quicker

The icicle on the aqueduct. (Vaughan Williams)

to go over the aqueduct. We'd start out from [Fron] at about quarter past eight and we'd be there for nine.

Audrey Owens, born 1938

The icicle

Vaughan took a photo of the icicle on the aqueduct. It was a very sunny February half term, must have been around fifteen years ago. We returned the following day and it had gone. The only proof was the ice on the ground below.

Julie Williams, born 1954

Not that path

When our boys were little, our next-door neighbour came in and she said, 'Mrs Diggory, could you have a word with your boys when they come home?' 'Why, what are they up to?' I said. So she said, 'I don't want to say any more, just have a word.' So the three of them came in … they were always about the wood and the aqueduct and so forth. 'Where have you been?' I said. 'Oh,' they said, 'We've been on the aqueduct.' So I said, 'Have you been throwing stones? What have you been doing?' 'Nothing.' 'Nothing?' I said, 'Well, Mrs Griffiths has been here and complained about the three of you. So I want to know just exactly what you were doing.' 'We were only walking along the aqueduct.' So I said, 'She wouldn't come here and complain if you were only walking along the path.' 'Oh, well, it wasn't that path, it was that one' – which was the girder, and they'd been walking along there. The outside of the trough! 'I won't have you doing that again,' I said, 'Or you'll be in trouble.'

Patricia Diggory, born 1924

Dares

As teenagers, we used to walk across the aqueduct on the outside of the railings, we would walk the full length on the metal ledge on the outside of the railings as a dare, keeping our hands over the top rail. You don't think anything of it when you're wild and young, do you? Heights never bothered me anyway.

David Russell Roberts, born 1944

Into the aqueduct

Peter: When I first started in Monsanto in 1953, a lot of the men from Chirk came on bicycles and they'd cycle over there, coming to Monsanto.

Gary: They reckon they were going over that bridge at night when they were finishing in Monsanto, men from Fron, on bikes, you know, finishing ten o'clock you see, the afternoon shift, and they were going like the clappers across the bridge to get to the Aqueduct for a pint before they shut and some of them fell in the water – going that fast on their bikes!

Peter Wright, born 1936 and Gary Roberts, born 1945

Betty's bike

I used to work in Wrexham, so I used to cycle over to Trevor over the aqueduct, leave my bike at my aunt's and catch the bus to Wrexham. So this Monday night it was a bit windy and me and the bike went straight in the canal. But luckily it was Monday night and there were quite a few coming over the aqueduct to the Fron choir rehearsal, walking over, so a couple helped me out. I got home soaking wet and mother nearly had a heart attack. But one of the funny things was, my father was working at Monsanto's and he was on afternoons, so he'd gone to work. They had a machine in the canal house that could get bikes out of the canal. So as he was coming home they were lifting my bike out. So he arrives home and says, 'Oh, you'll never guess, someone's gone in the canal again!' Not realising that it was me. He didn't even recognise my bike! After that I don't think I rode my bike over again, I used to push it over the aqueduct. I wouldn't go all the way round by road; that was too much like hard work.

Betty Jones, born 1938

Saturday night ritual

There was [a] man from the village who used to fall in regular going home on a Saturday

Monsanto's bike sheds. (Flexsys archive)

night in Fron and one night he went home and he was sober this night, but on the way home he jumped in the canal and they said, 'What did you do that for?' He says, 'Well I normally fall in, so I thought I'd do it of my own accord tonight.' It was just his ritual on a Saturday night.

Karen Wright, born 1965

Jumping the aqueduct

I had an uncle that lived in the Fron, and if he'd had a drink he used to jump from one side to the other, on the aqueduct. He'd jump to the other side!

Gertrude Jones, born 1915

Dampened ardour

Bert Rowlands, he used to reckon – this is in 1915, 1920 – someone from the Fron was courting a girl here in Acrefair, and came to the Hampden Arms for a drink every Saturday night. First night going back – in the canal. Second Saturday night – in the canal. Third Saturday night – threw the bike in and jumped in after it. It was only 4ft deep but you can't get out because your feet go under the footpath. You've got to get to one end or the other to get out, you can't get out. The footpath is built out so much, when you try to get out it pushes your legs under and you can't get out.

Peter Wright, born 1936

Scotch Hall Bridge

As we got to our teenage years, we would go up to Scotch Hall Bridge. The boys from Fron would come along the aqueduct and we'd get together. But the boys from Newbridge would go to Fron, to look for the girls there. A lot of us found husbands and the boys found wives, we used to say 'from across the bridge'! I met my husband on the Scotch Hall Bridge and he invited me to the pictures in Cefn, in the Palace.

Betty James, born 1922

The man from the Pru

My mother and father met on the aqueduct. My father's father worked at the Prudential and my father did. And my grandfather was moved up to Cefn and he went into digs with my great-grandmother. He went to chapel on the Sunday with my great-grandmother. My mother was one of six children, you see, and they all came to chapel, all these girls. He wrote to my father and said, 'I've seen the girl I want you to marry!' Which was my mother, who he saw in chapel. My father was living in South Wales and he came up on holiday and he went to my great-grandmother's, who he didn't know at all and said, 'Well, where are they?' 'Oh, well, they're on the Sunday School trip.' So he came down to the basin, you know, to wait for the big boat to come. And they came, because his parents must have been on the boat, mustn't they, my grandparents, and my mother and her sisters and all of them. And then, so he said, he fell in love with my mother as soon as he saw her. And she wouldn't marry him for ten years, you know. She was twenty, and she was twenty-nine when they got married. She wouldn't go to live, you see, in South Wales, she wouldn't leave the family. And when she married him, he used to say she used to cry all the way to Cardiff and in the end she only cried to Chirk. My mother and father were ... born a month between them and a year younger than the year, so they were born in 1901.

Iola Roberts, born 1933

A view of the aqueduct from Pentre. (Joe and Brenda Little)

The wedding of Iola Roberts' parents, Glanville and Celia, c. 1930. (Iola Roberts)

Flyboats

At the far end of Trevor Docks there used to stand a warehouse, quite a substantial building, and the canal used to run directly into this building to enable boats to be loaded and unloaded. When the canal was a major means of transportation, there were special boats which carried perishable merchandise. These boats were called flyboats and they had right of way over other traffic on the canal. They travelled twenty-four hours a day and carried all kinds of goods to the warehouse. In one part of the warehouse an ice-breaking boat was maintained and this was used for breaking up the ice which formed on the aqueduct.

Emrys Roberts, born 1922

Scarecrow

Some boys hung a scarecrow up, hung it off the bridge you know, and the people in Froncysyllte saw it and of course they must have thought somebody had hung himself. I was one of the boys by the way. A foolish thing to do, but it startled the people all right.

Cecil Diggory, born 1920

A being of sorts

My father, Raymond Jones, had been with Air Products on a trip to Blackpool when he was a young lad, when he lived in Fron. He was walking home from Cefn one night along the aqueduct and it was dark. As he was walking along, he wanted a cigarette, but he hadn't got a light. He could see a man in the middle of the aqueduct wearing dark clothes and a strange-shaped hat and he stopped and asked him for a light. He didn't speak to him, this man, he just offered my Dad a light for his cigarette. My Dad took a couple of paces past and turned round and went to say, 'Thanks, goodnight' and the man had gone and my Dad apparently ran all the way home, which was uphill! Didn't stop running until he got to the house and that's another true story. He's adamant it was in the middle of the aqueduct and there was no way that man could have gone either way to get to the end of the aqueduct and he hadn't heard a splash, so he always thinks he met a being of sorts that night!

Karen Wright, born 1965

Pontycysyllte Aqueduct. (Emrys Roberts)

seven

Village Life

Mary's Acre

Acrefair is Mary's Acre and one of the local historians suggested that it was St Mary, and that it was associated with St Mary's parish church in Ruabon. Acrefair in translation: 'Acre' is acre, 'fair' is a mutation of Mair, Mary. So Acrefair is Mary's Acre. Now, there was a new estate went up in Acrefair, off Bethania Road, that was called Mountain View. Why it was called Mountain View I've no idea: I'm sure they couldn't see a mountain for miles around because they were all so closely packed together. When the powers-that-be ruled us from Shire Hall in Mold, they had this anathema for anything English, so they immediately thought; Acrefair – which they translated as 'Acre Fair' – in the middle of everything else Welsh, they assumed it was English, and translated it as Erw Deg – sunny or fair acre. So we've got this estate now, off Bethania Road, called Erw Deg, which is completely wrong.

The Acre, I've read, came from the Abbot: he used to bestow lettings and things, and the Abbot in Valle Crucis parcelled out the land, and if you'd been very, very good and saintly, or whatever, they gave you an acre. And this Mary somewhere, must have done something for the church.

Bob Watkin, born 1930

Number 9 Maelor Terrace

My husband was from Acrefair. I always knew him, I suppose. I used to go to the Congregational church in Cefn, and the minister we had then was the Reverend H.S. Cresswell, and he lived next door to Harry and his father and mother. And we used to go to the same birthday parties, as kids. And then we had a Young People's Guild in Hill Street, and we both attended that. He was in India for four years, in the RAF, in the war. And

Mile End, Acrefair. (Arthur and Barbara Humphries)

then when he came back, well we struck up a friendship, and it went on from there. Our first house was in Maelor Terrace, in Acrefair, No. 9 Maelor Terrace. We were married on 9 August, and our first house was No. 9, which was a coincidence, wasn't it?

Kathleen Smith, born 1923

Tŷ Brith

Tŷ Brith is 'speckled or mottled house', and whereas it's red brick, it's got here and there grey bricks – now whether they ran out of red bricks, I don't know! Joshua Powell, along with his brother-in-law, built this house and the one that's attached, and they brought the bricks up by the railway line, which runs along the bottom of the wall, and threw them down the bank, and then built the houses from those. That was the railway line that came from Trevor station, almost via J.C. Edwards, and it came up to Monsanto. When I was a little girl, the train used to go up very regularly, they used to take coal to the powerhouse and the train went up four times a day, if not more, a little steam train. It was very much a regular thing in my childhood. You knew when the train was coming and you went out to wave to the driver.

Diane Powell, born 1946

We don't move far

I was born in Rhosymedre and I came to live here [Acrefair] when I was three. Joshua lived here and died at eighty-six and his one daughter, my grandfather's sister, she lived with him. My Powell grandparents lived next door but one. We don't move very far! I've realised since I took early retirement and been dog walking, there is still quite a community feeling about the place. If people don't know me, they know the dog!

Diane Powell, born 1946

Diane Powell's great-grandfather Joshua with his second wife and children. The baby is Diane's grandfather. This photograph is from a tin negative. (Diane Powell)

School stamps

The post office in Acrefair was where Mr Sharma has his shop. There used to be a path down from the school, and then you crossed on the zebra crossing. The people who kept the post office – well he had the barber's shop, Emrys Tompkinson. Tony, who has the barber's shop now, he served his apprenticeship with Emrys Tompkinson. His wife, and his mother-in-law, kept the post office. Everybody always referred to her as Nanny. You went into the post office and it was all dark wood. She used to open this little grill. We used to be sent there to buy National Savings stamps. They had pictures of Prince Charles and Princess Anne on them, as young children. Prince Charles was on the half a crown, and Princess Anne was on the sixpenny one. You would be sent with the total of money to get the school stamps for that day. Can you imagine it now? We were really proud, if we were chosen.

Diane Powell, born 1946

Acrefair School

I've lived in Acrefair the biggest part of my life. I went to Acrefair School – there's an empty patch of ground opposite, that's where the Acrefair boys', girls' and infants' was. That's the school I went to, and then to Ruabon Grammar School. All those buildings have gone down now. Oh, I can remember what it was like there. I enjoyed junior school very much, more I think than grammar school.

Betty Thompson, born 1922

The boundary

I live near Darkie Wood. It would have been built when the railway was built. It's a tunnel that's got a pathway thrown out on wood over the water, going the length of the tunnel. It's quite romantic you know. It's a magnet for children, because you can play Poohsticks there. It's the nant of Trefynant and it's the boundary between Acrefair and Trevor. It goes right under the road, by the Duke. It goes down eventually past the Mill pub and there used to be a mill opposite the pub. The old turnpike road used to go along there. The turnpike goes up beside the bed shop, it comes out in Bethania Road, then it comes out on the Llangollen road, but we don't know what happens to it after that.

Edward Jones, born 1937

Saturday night

The place to be on Friday and Saturday nights in those days was Cefn Mawr. It was like Piccadilly Circus, there were hundreds, yes hundreds of people there. People from Newbridge, Garth, Trevor, Fron, Rhosymedre, Ruabon – and Cefn of course – gathered there. There were two cinemas each showing films at 5.30 and 8.00 – queues of people stretching past the Holly Bush and down Hill Street, umpteen pubs and shops doing business quite late at night. On Saturday nights there used to be a man who set up his stall to sell crockery and earthenware goods on a patch of ground between the Holly Bush and Vaults – he may have been from the Staffordshire area. He had considerable competition from the local Salvation Army band and songsters, who assembled in front of the Vaults. The band in those days was quite a sizeable one – I have a vivid picture in my mind of the scene and the noise and bustle of those times.

Emrys Roberts, born 1922

Shops in Cefn

There were lots and lots of shops in Cefn, there was no need to go to town, which is the opposite now, you've got to go to town, because you've only got Kwik Save really.

Pete Garrett, born 1949

Melias and Gracies

In Cefn there was marvellous shops ... Melias, Gracies and the lot. We'd go from here to Cefn to the pictures and the buses would be packed, you'd be standing on them! But they used to have such wonderful shops in Cefn: Watkin Williamson's and things like that. Morris's shop, in the far end of Cefn, he was the one that sold shoes, and then he had another department where he sold hardware stuff and stuff like that. We used to think it was marvellous going to Morris's for shoes. And then you'd go to Gracies. I remember one Christmas, I wanted a short coat, they were the fashion then and my mother said oh, she couldn't, but Christmas morning I got the short coat, and it was from Gracies in Cefn. And of course next door was Melias, which was a big food store then, like Tesco's or something today, and you'd have the lot there.

Audrey Owens, born 1938

The entrance to Trefynant Park, 1950s. (Howard Paddock)

Crane Street, Cefn. (David Russell Roberts)

Janet Williams' great-nain and great-taid on the steps outside the cottage where Janet still lives. (Janet Williams)

Butcher's shop

There used to be a butcher's shop down by where the post office is; they hadn't got any electricity or gas, all they'd got was a flame. It wouldn't be allowed these days. They didn't have fridges or anything and so they used to have to sell off the meat.

Rhona Roberts, born 1928

The March Fair

In March each year the famous travelling fairs visited Cefn Mawr to attract even greater throngs of people. They pitched their main attractions on Cefn Bank – now a car park – but some of their booths and caravans spilled out onto the Crane and down past the Railway pub. It was unforgettable, with showmen's steam engines, brightly coloured lights and fairground organs making the village a very lively place. I am told there were times past when caged wild animals were part of the scene, but that was before my time. However, I just about remember very faintly the boxing booths which were part of the fair. Any man in the audience was invited to enter the ring for three rounds – for a small fee of course – against the professional boxer and hope to last the fight. I should imagine that many of the contestants had got sufficient ale down them to give them the necessary courage. Cefn was a colourful, dynamic place in those times.

Emrys Roberts, born 1922

My cottage

The cottage I live in is probably one of the oldest in the village [of Cefn]. It's two up, two down, literally you walk from one bedroom to the other and the walls are about six feet thick. So it's a very, very old house. It used to be a smallholding and our family have lived here for many, many years. It was rented originally from the Wynnstay estate, because the house had passed into their ownership, like a lot of properties in this area, and my great-grandfather bought it during the war. So that's when they finally owned it.

Janet Williams, born 1965

Stone remains

There was a house I remember at the top of Cefn, when I was a boy, and it had a plaque above the window: R. and M. Paddock, 1813. Now that stone is on a garden wall, in the top of Cefn. The house has been demolished. But the stone is still there.

Howard Paddock, born 1944

Temple Vale

I've lived in this house about thirty-six years. Mr Templeton had this house, that's why they call it Temple Vale. Penybont brick, you know, and there was no road, it was only a dirt track. My father-in-law had an allotment. He used to say to me, 'Bring a bucket, later on, and I'll give you some potatoes!' I used to come all the way down here with a bucket and I used to have all the little teeny potatoes. And I had a funny mother-in-law. 'Don't you tell her!' he used to say to me, 'Don't you tell her!'

Gertrude Jones, born 1915

My first home

You come down this very long flight of steps, then you come down a short flight, and the surgery was there, and then there was a row of houses, and our house, Plas Kynaston Terrace, was the first one. I presume because of the surgery, it was always referred to as the doctor's steps.

Kathleen Smith, born 1923

Froncysyllte Basin. (Betty Jones)

Plas Kynaston

When I was a boy, the library was in the hall of Plas Kynaston. It had a particularly unusual staircase: the steps came out of the wall and are not supported, they're sort of wedged in the wall, there's nothing to support them. I think the old staircase may well be a listed feature. It certainly was unusual.

Howard Paddock, born 1944

Cefn stone

[Plas Kynaston has] an unsupported staircase. They're all Cefn stone slabs, projecting from the wall one after the other, there's no support the other side. You wonder how they can be safe; they've been worn so much. The servants' quarters were at the back and behind the wall

there was an orchard, which came all the way down. It was an L-shaped building, there was a back projection.

Bob Watkin, born 1930

Cefn station

It was quite a busy station. The stationmaster used to wear a cap with gold braid and brass buttons on his coat. We had a booking office with a clerk, and two porters. We went everywhere on the train; the buses hadn't started to run then. We used to go on what they called 'on the motor': it was a small train which had two long carriages. It had got wooden slat seats in it and if we wanted to go to Wrexham or Ruabon, or even Gobowen to go to Oswestry, we would go on the motor. Then after a while the Midland Red buses started to go through.

Betty James, born 1922

Cefn was a smell

Cefn was a smell – the pungent odour of Monsanto that hung on the air and took three days to get used to – a dustiness – even grass blades and shiny red bricks seemed somehow coated with black – and a sense of dangerous edges, even from the foot of my Gran's garden, where you could tumble down a mountain and break your neck. But it was also a friendly place, where I was Emily Bluck's first granddaughter in a tribe that produced lads.

Pauline (Polly) Bluck, born 1952

Lizzie Cabbage

There was Jack Alma at the very far end, which sold a bit of everything. You come along the village [Froncysyllte] and there was the Co-op, which has just been made into flats. A little bit lower down the road was the chip shop. Then coming along where the shop is empty now they sold papers, it was a newsagent's. Then a little bit higher up, bottom of the steps was a butcher's. Cross the road by that broken down shop now: that was a pet shop. Then coming along we had the post office and that was a big shop as well. Then across the road was the hairdresser's and another butcher's. Then on the corner where these flats are now was a draper's, sold everything. Then across the road where the Indian is was another newsagent's and bric-a-brac. And then halfway up the street, up the hill was a saddler. Then of course the fruit man used come around, Bob the Barrow, and Bob the Breadman used to come around with bread. I can remember the milkman coming around

with the milk in urns, with horses and traps. You used to go with a jug to get the milk out of the urns. On the top, where we lived, there was a little shop we used to call Auntie Lizzie Cabbage, she sold everything. Lizzie the Cabbage, her shop was a tin shed. The sweets there were wonderful, all the old sweets. She had everything. She was what I call a real old lady. She was lovely; she was really a nice lady. She was dressed up in her cape, a crocheted cape, all in black, long black skirts and sometimes a fawny one. She had the old boots. Of course years ago most of the people had, not nicknames, but you'd know people as Mr Jones yr Ochr and Bob the Barrow, Bob the Breadman, Will Kendrick the Milkman.

Audrey Owens, born 1938

The Co-op

The Co-op was there, there was a butcher's, a hairdresser's. There was a lot more shops than there is now. The chapels were there – there were four chapels and a church then and all that's left is the church. There is one chapel there, but I don't think they have many services – the chapel is used for funerals.

Betty Jones, born 1938

Memorial fountain

My grandfather's home was in Froncysyllte and his brother was killed in the Boer War. He was a bachelor, my great-uncle. He never married. You know the memorial fountain in the Fron? There were two of them from the Fron, they were both killed in the Boer War. They've moved the fountain now and there were two drinking cups, but somebody took them.

Gertrude Jones, born 1915

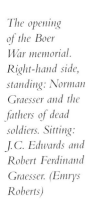

The opening of the Boer War memorial. Right-hand side, standing: Norman Graesser and the fathers of dead soldiers. Sitting: J.C. Edwards and Robert Ferdinand Graesser. (Emrys Roberts)

Gas lamps

Fron was quite a nice little place, and because Mr Graesser was so influential, he was director of the Gas Board in Cefn, so we had gas in Fron ahead of everyone else, and we had street gas lamps. It used to be lovely.

Dennis Williams, born 1931

256 children

The total school roll in the late 1920s was 256 children. This number of children is an indication of the size of the population of Fron in those days – probably something of the order of 1,200 persons. To support a population of this size – especially when car ownership and public transport were virtually nonexistent – warranted the need for numerous shops, places of worship, pubs and other facilities in Fron.

Emrys Roberts, born 1922

Saturday night

Fron was very much a mining community in those days, they mostly worked in Black Park Colliery, but there were many other collieries in the area. On a Saturday night they used to

do a lot of fighting and I used to listen to these raised voices and it used to frighten me a bit, when you're a kid. The village is so quiet now, compared with what it used to be.

Dennis Williams, born 1931

Married in the Baptist chapel

I got married in 1953. I got married in the chapel... it's been pulled down now. The Baptist Chapel up on the top. [I got married in] just a cream dress, and you had your reception, the ladies of the chapel got together and made you a buffet in the vestry and that was all. But we had a happy life. We had a little cottage along the road. We used to take the nappies and had a fire boiler outside and then put them on the line – no washing machines then! You were still in the village, still with your friends and with your family. I never missed a day when I didn't go and visit my mother, like.

Audrey Owens, born 1938

Tramps

My grandfather had a coal business in Fron. You can almost see where the old wharf was. He lived in a house by the canal and then they had the wharf – there's the drawbridge, a path into Fron and there's a house there, in latter years it was the doctor's surgery, that's the house, and then along there was the wharf where they used to bring the coal on the boats. Further on was the lime works. There used to be quite a few tramps about then, but they weren't any bother and they weren't dangerous. They used to come almost once a year, the same men. They'd come into my grandfather's yard, my grandmother would give them food. They'd never go in the house; they'd sit outside. Sometimes they'd go into the bottom of where the lime works was, it was warm there in the night. My grandfather was a foreman, after he gave the coal business up, he was a foreman on the lime works and he found one dead there one morning. Mr Williams, that owned and ran the lime works, buried him; they didn't know if he had any family or anything. They didn't know where he was from, so he was buried in Fron. It was in the paper at the time.

Betty Jones, born 1938

They stopped overnight in Fron

The tramps used to travel between the work-houses. Fron was a halfway point between Morda and Corwen workhouses so they stopped overnight in Fron, by the lime kilns for warmth. One of the poor tramps in the middle of winter died at the lime kilns and he was buried at St David's in Fron, December 1910.

Emrys Roberts, born 1922

Tom the Post's lad

I grew up in Garth. My father was the postman. I was 'Tom the Post's lad'. I didn't have a name! I was always 'Tom the Post's lad'. We weren't supervised as children are now in the playground but we wouldn't

dream of running away or playing truant because everybody knew everybody then. You almost couldn't play truant because some-body's parent would spot you and they'd say, 'Why aren't you in school, Edward?' Things like that. It was a rural community, it policed itself, if you know what I mean. I mean, there was a truant officer but there was only one for the whole Wrexham area, because it was almost unknown.

Edward Jones, born 1937

Cerrig Llithrig

Cerrig Llithrig was a farm and Lena Lloyd's grandmother lived until she was ninety and lived there. School Hill in Garth – I hate coming down that hill, there's a bend right on the bottom as well. Instead of coming round that bend, you went right, and that's Cerrig Llithrig. There's a little cottage there, and the Safety Officer for Wales built a house there. The house they built was called Tan y Dderwen. They don't live there anymore. But they had the house built, brand new, because I remember going up there. Garth has altered tremendously. There's a remnant of a lane, but that's all. Well, it's sixty-odd years ago.

Members of Cefn Past and Present Local History Group

Stone cottages

I grew up in the 1920s, early 1930s, and Newbridge was a village mostly of small stone cottages, a few red-brick houses. There were a lot of children in the village then, about 155 that I could think about. There were large families. We were all the same, our fathers worked either in the brickyard or in the collieries. We didn't have very much, but we made the best of what we had.

Betty James, born 1922

A view of Newbridge from Pentre. (David Russell Roberts)

They sold practically everything

Newbridge was quite a big village. There was the Co-op shop, just below what was Cefn station. There was the Waterloo shop, and then they built the shop which is now a bungalow. But the old Waterloo building is still there. And we had a post office, there were two chip shops, a cobbler's shop, a barber's, four sweet shops, that were open all hours; they sold practically everything in these shops. We had two butchers, a greengrocer with a horse and cart, five pubs and two chapels. Nowadays, traders don't go around like we had: the greengrocers coming around with fish and vegetables, and the baker from Cefn – there's no baker's there now – coming around with bread in the van. They used to come two days a week. Even the pot man used to come around at one time, selling pots and soap – toilet soaps. I suppose they think everyone's got a car, and they can shop further afield.

Betty James, born 1922

No traffic

There was no traffic, there were no buses running. Only Pete's of Oswestry had an old traction engine, and that would come through every day, they would go to the docks at Birkenhead, for grain. That was all; otherwise it was all horse and trap, just the odd bicycle and motorcycle. On a Wednesday we would sit on the field and watch the farmers driving the cattle home from Oswestry, the cattle they'd bought that morning. They walked all the way home, with the dogs and the cattle.

Betty James, born 1922

Grazing goats

Some of my brothers and sisters were allergic to cows' milk and what we had to do was get goats. Before all the rules and regulations came … you had the land coming down from the railway track at a slope and then it levelled off level with the top of the wall. The farmers used the grass for hay, they used to come and cut and gather the hay each summer. When we ran out of grass in the garden we'd put the goat on the railway embankment to graze. I'm not sure if somebody put other animals there, but I think there were.

Sonia T. Benbow-Jones, born 1943

Shortcut to Whitehurst

If you were going to Whitehurst it was the norm to jump onto the wall, go up the side of the railway bridge, that big bridge going under to Bro Gwilym, climb onto the railway track and use that as the shortcut to Whitehurst. If a train came you just stood against the wall and tried not to look the driver in the eye because he'd be shaking his fist at you.

Sonia T. Benbow-Jones, born 1943

Wynnstay Park

During the school holidays we always used to go down to the river to play. That's where we learnt to swim, in the river, on the grove, or else we would go down to the park and trespass on the island, and spend the day there, in Wynnstay Park. Sir Watkin used to come on horseback and if we were playing in the road, he used to stand by the wall and chat and ask us not to go into the park. Then, in the 1930s, Mr Arthur Hughes – he was the councillor for Newbridge – approached Sir Watkin, [asking] if he could make an opening in the wall for the children of Newbridge to enjoy the Wynnstay Park. And that's what he did. And it was a wonderful time for the children. We used to go and get chestnuts and when the bluebells were out, it was beautiful.

Betty James, born 1922

Children of Newbridge

You never had to lock the doors; you never had to worry about things. We had the park to play in because there was a letter that Mr Arthur had from the Wynnstay estate, which gave the children of Newbridge access to the park. I think it was to stop at the end of the war but we still claimed it as our village right. So we had dens, we had swings and with the old prams we used to make trolleys and have trolley runs. We used to go down to the river Dee. You went over the new bridge and down the side past the water bailiff's cottage and there's a nice area of flat land and we used to build campfires there so we could cook. We used to make rafts – always put the youngest on to see if the raft would sink because, after all, you want the youngest ones getting wet, not the older ones. We could go fishing there. We also used to go over the railway line, drop down before you got to Whitehurst and go to the canal. You could fish for eels in the canal – very, very meaty, very nutritious. If you went up over the railway by Newbridge and then straight down behind the back of Cefn Bychan Chapel there was a wonderful daffy bank. If you went through the Wynnstay Park there was a wonderful daffy bank. At the top of Cae Gwilym Lane was the remnants of the Plas Kynaston mines and you had the shaley mine deposit and there were a lot of pussy willows. I used to get a bunch of pussy willows and then go and pick the daffs and go home with a nice bunch for Mummy, especially if I'd been doing something wrong. If I'd ripped my clothes because I'd been climbing trees, or I could get through a pair of shoes in a month, so I needed to sweeten the fact that the sole was off my shoe, or the sleeve was ripped out of my new blazer or I'd got a rip in a skirt.

Sonia T. Benbow-Jones, born1943

Rhosymedre

Rhosymedre as a village was a nice compact little village and it could be safely said that

Whitehurst toll-house on the A5. (Arthur and Barbara Humphries)

The Monsanto water bailiff in a coracle on the river Dee, 1960s. (Flexsys archive)

Wynnstay Hall. (Arthur and Barbara Humphries)

one knew everyone; sadly, not today. The village finished at The Points, Park Road, Rhosymedre, the Plas Isaf estate being added at a later date. There's a large stone house in Brook Street, where an engineer, Mr Lloyd Jones, who was employed by Sir Watkin, lived, and further on was just another cottage. I can remember Brook Street being flooded because of the brook, and sand bags all along the street. So there was Brook Street, Church Street, Chapel Street, Rock Road and part of Park Road, up to The Points; that was the end of Rhosymedre. There were four public houses: the Anchor, which is no longer there, the Co-operative Society bought that to extend their warehouse – the Bowling Green was the true name of it but people called it the Anchor – the Eagles, now Park View nursing home, the Plough and Jolly Masons, known as the top house.

I think people felt more secure than they do now. A policeman was based right in Rhosymedre itself. The police station, when I was younger, was in a row of stone houses in the High Street. The policeman lived in one of those houses. Mr Davis, his name was. And of course, we had a bowling green, tennis courts belonging to the Co-operative Society – so very well catered for – church, three chapels and pubs as well.

Rhona Roberts, born 1928

Funeral director

Where you come over the bridge in Church Street there used to be an enormous tin hut and a workshop and they made all these coffins. And they had this old vehicle, the hearse. They even had a horse-drawn hearse. I never saw it in action but he had it in the garage. He was the only funeral director around here. That was Herbert Cardon.

Pete Garrett, born 1949

The Co-op

When I started work, I worked in the head office of the Co-operative Society, where the Wheatsheaf workshops are now. It had twenty-one branches in the district. One could say that Rhosymedre, as a village, was quite self-contained because one could get anything one wanted in the Co-operative Society building. There was a ladies' department, gents' outfitting, shoes, hardware, the bakery and the dairy, and a shoe repair place. When it closed it made a terrific difference to the village. The shops used to be open quite late, which lit up High Street.

Rhona Roberts, born 1928

The hill

You don't realise how much has gone but virtually half the hill has disappeared and is now in the aqueduct and the viaduct and lots of stone cottages as far away as Liverpool, and there's a big hall in Liverpool, by Central station, St George's Hall – it's famous for its dance floor. That's where it's all gone. And probably it built Wynnstay Hall because that's all Cefn sandstone, and the tower here, Waterloo Tower.

Pete Garrett, born 1949

The collieries

The Wynnstay Colliery was always known as the Green Colliery round here. And that closed about 1927, so it's been shut a long time. At one time it was a full-scale colliery. There were lots of pits and slag heaps. Opposite the Caravan Centre, all that piece of land that's now an industrial estate, that was all one enormous red tip, hundreds of feet high. Reddish, definitely a reddish colour.

Pete Garrett, born 1949

Plough Corner, Park Road, Rhosymedre. (Arthur and Barbara Humphries)

Wynnstay Colliery, 1920. (Arthur and Barbara Humphries)

Cefn sandstone

Most of the men worked in the collieries and Penybont brickworks and Monsanto, and when I was in school, the quarry itself was producing Cefn sandstone, and we'd hear the shots, breaking the sandstone. Cefn is famous for its sandstone. The church is built of Cefn sandstone.

Rhona Roberts, born 1928

Rhosymedre church

Rhosymedre church is dedicated to St John the Evangelist. It was consecrated on 6 July 1837. Tradition has it that round about that period, before the church was built, the then Sir Watkin Williams Wynne was passing by and saw a group of people within the area where the church is now, having an outdoor service. So he was one of the great benefactors of the church and enabled it to be built. Rhosymedre church has got quite a famous name because there is a hymn tune entitled 'Rhosymedre' written by the first vicar of Rhosymedre, the Reverend J.D. Edwards. It's a well-known tune and Vaughan Williams the composer has composed on the tune itself a piece of music. Of course, what Rhosymedre church is quite noted for is the fine example of tiles around the altar, which were made by members of this church and

St Paul's church, Acrefair, who worked in the Trefynant works, in memory of James Coster Edwards. These tiles are reckoned to be one of the finest examples of this type in the country, so we do have quite a few visitors coming to it. The east window is dedicated in Sir Watkin's memory and there's another window in church dedicated to Queen Victoria. It is a Grade II listed building, mainly because of the tiles.

Rhona Roberts, born 1928

Curing epilepsy

One of the traditions of the local people, round about the 1800s, was that if they suffered from epilepsy and went to the vicar and asked for a silver coin from the offertory, which had been blessed, and had it made into a silver ring, that this would cure epilepsy. Of course, we don't know whether that's true or not, do we?

Rhona Roberts, born 1928

Some of the altar tiles in Rhosymedre church. (Amy Douglas)

Trevor boatyard

It was originally called Hill's boatyard and the man in charge was Mr Fisher. I don't know why it lost that name.

Cecil Diggory, born 1920

Trevor foundry

The foundry was across the road from the canal, Trevor foundry. There's three houses built on it now. My father owned that foundry and my grandfather before him, and some of the railings were made in that foundry, for the path on the towpath. A lot of people don't know that but I do. It was a firm from London that owned it then, I believe, but my grandad bought it after.

Cecil Diggory, born 1920

Forges, factories and foundries

People often ask me, 'Where was this foundry, where the aqueduct was cast?' At Trevor Basin, that was more of a blacksmith's than a foundry. They never really cast things there. It ended up as a scrapyard and then it was closed, and they built three very big houses there. If you look at old maps, you'll see that marked on there; sometimes they call it a factory. Turns out that they called forges 'factories'. When the Industrial Revolution started, there were hundreds of these forges. If you looked across from Fron, you'd see all the fires, at night. They'd make their pig iron and then it was picked up and processed, in one big place, and that was Plas Kynaston, and then it grew. They cast the troughs for the aqueduct.

Edward Jones, born 1937

The Telford Inn

The Telford Inn, which was Scotch Hall, was where Telford lived when he worked on the aqueduct. At the end of the bridge, the end of the Pont as we call it, there's a smaller building which was the place where the bargees paid their fees to him, paying for the rights of being on the canal.

Cecil Diggory, born 1920

Trevor station

My mother-in-law used to tell the tale: one of her sisters came from Manchester and they were going to go to Barmouth for the day. So they went down to the station, to get on the train, and the chap on the station, Ellis, was there and he said to my mother-in-law, 'Mrs Diggory, it looks like rain. You haven't got an umbrella.' So she said, 'No, we'll be all right.' But he said, 'No, no, no.' So she said, 'Well, the train's coming,' and he said, 'Never mind, I'll hold it up, go and get your umbrella.' So of course she only had to go up the steps and across the road to the house and she came back with her umbrella. Well, Auntie Louie couldn't get over it. She used to tell everybody, 'They stop the trains in Wales for Ginnie!'

Patricia Diggory, born 1924

Dick's Shop

We would call in Dick's Shop with our pennies, or take bottles back to the shop to get the money back and buy sweets or lucky bags. You could buy anything – or so it seemed – from Dick's Shop: one egg, one Beecham's Powder, Senior Service or Player's cigarettes for my grandad. And of course the rows of sweets in jars. Pineapple chunks were a favourite.

Julie Williams, born 1954

Trevor station, September 1965. (Pete Garrett)

The Dolydd

As children, we would walk down the steep path at the side of Dick's Shop. I was only allowed to go down the Dolydd if my brother was going too. And we were both warned not to go near the river! I'm sure that's why to this day I can't swim. If I'd gone into the river with the other children, I would have had more confidence in water. We used to walk through the field full of cows down to a rope swing on a big tree and swing over the edge of the river. We would be out for the day and often walked up to the field next to Trevor Basin, where there were swings.

Julie Williams, born 1954

Great-taid's tools

When my great-taid passed away, he had some tools that were gathering dust in the corner and my nanna and my taid didn't know what to do with them. So they decided to donate them where people could see them, and they donated them to Tŷ Mawr and they're still there now, hanging up in the barn and there's a little plaque with my great-taid's name on it.

Ben Jones, born 1993

Potato scales

When I was a child, I lived not far from Tŷ Mawr, which was then a farm, and I used to take the 'peelings' to the farm for the pigs. They would be in the field on the left-hand side, where the entrance is now, and I would lean on my elbows on the wall with my legs dangling and watch the pigs come running for their scraps of peelings. I remember going to the farmhouse to buy potatoes. I can still picture the huge potato scales in the porch and the farmer's wife in her wrapover pinny.

Julie Williams, born 1954

Dolydd, near the aqueduct. (David Russell Roberts)

The Parrys

I remember Tŷ Mawr, when it was a farm. I remember the Parrys there, years and years ago. I lived in Newbridge when I was young; I used to look after my aunt. And there was nothing on there – I used to bring the dog for a walk on the bank. All those houses, by Tŷ Mawr, have been built since, haven't they?

Gertrude Jones, born 1915

War potatoes

During the war, Mr Jones, who was the farmer in Tŷ Mawr, would come around and he'd ask, 'Would you like to have a row of potatoes in the field?' Five shillings, it was then. It would be twenty-five pence now. So he would plant

DONATED BY
THE LATE GEORGE PHILLIPS
OF CEFN MAWR
GRATEFUL THANKS TO
HIS FAMILY

Above: *Ben Jones with the farming tools donated to Tŷ Mawr by his great-grandfather, George Phillips. (Alasdair Thomson)*

Right: *George Phillips working the land that is now part of Tŷ Mawr Country Park. (Ann Jones)*

the potatoes under the arches of the viaduct. In the autumn he would come and say, 'The potatoes are ready for rising.' So we'd all go down with sacks and you'd pick the potatoes up and you'd have enough potatoes to last for the winter.

Betty James, born 1922

Fetching the milk

After school, we would go down to Tŷ Mawr to fetch the milk with a can with a handle on; a milk can. One in each hand: one for my grandmother, one for us. There would be a lot of children there and perhaps the cows would just be coming up from the field. So we'd go into the shippon and watch them milking. We'd have the milk and it would be hot. It wasn't sterilised or anything. During the summer, Mrs Jones, the housekeeper, would say, 'Tell your grandmother I've made butter.' So we'd have to go back then, to fetch butter. Oh, it was lovely.

Betty James, born 1922

Sledging

We used to sledge in Back Field because we had a field that was big enough to go sledging on, so my friends used to come and we used to sledge there. Certainly when I was working [in Tŷ Mawr Country Park], when we had a real good do of snow, it would be this bank … it would be full of people sliding down on anything from a plastic bag to an upturned car roof.

Janet Williams, born 1965

In my nightie!

I've been all around Tŷ Mawr. Animals and things there. Safe, isn't it, there? I know a friend, a great friend of mine. I was ready for bed in my nightie and dressing gown and she came running over to take me for a walk round there. I said, 'I'm in my nightie!' She said, 'Don't worry, we'll put a shawl round you.' And she took me for a couple of hours. In my nightie! Nobody knew I was in it. Lovely weather. There's a big bridge there, somewhere. We went right by it but we didn't cross over it … went in the chair I did. Seen the ducks and the pigeons and the rabbits, and those ugly pigs.

Dolly Edwards, born 1915

eight

Local Characters

Crad the Garth

He was a character, there's no doubt about it. He used to stop traffic on the road, and he used to say, 'I'll show you where the mountains are, half a crown,' and he'd jump in, and he'd take them up the road, up to Panorama. It was amazing the number of people who would stop and allow him to get in the car. I remember one stopping and a fist came out ... and hit Crad there, between the eyes. I remember a friend of mine, he was a seaman, he'd been at sea for many years and he was up in the Arctic Circle somewhere on his boat and this chap said to him, 'Where do you come from?' 'I come from North Wales,' he said. 'Where in North Wales?' 'Oh,' he said, 'You wouldn't know it, it's a little village called Trevor.' 'Oh,' he said, 'do you know Crad the Garth?' Oh aye, he was well known!

Cecil Diggory, born 1920, and Patricia Diggory, born 1924

Uncle Willy

My Uncle Willy, he was a blacksmith by day and a poacher by night! He was caught one night in Chirk Castle estate and he ran away and they chased him. They were building Bont Chapel at the bottom there, so he got hold of a spade ... and he was working and the men didn't know that he wasn't a workman there. He was as crafty as that, he was a monkey, he was.

Cecil Diggory, born 1920

Ben the bookie's runner

Ben Tailor was the bookie's runner, because betting was illegal then, and he was a dapper little man. He lived in the Forge Row. He would start by the Tally Ho and he would creep up the hill by the wall and he would look to see if there was any sign of the policeman, and then he would dash into one of the houses and he would collect the betting slips for the day. If you had a betting slip, you'd put a nom de plume on it and he'd know you by your nom de plume. He'd look down the list to see if you'd got any money coming back, if you'd done a horse the day before, and then he would push the slip inside his hat, inside the band, and then he'd look up and down the road again, and then he's be off again, going to another house, to collect the slips. I think he was caught once or twice but he didn't go to jail. I think the bookies must have paid his fine. Another job he used to do, he would come around first thing in the morning with a big overcoat on and he'd knock the door and he'd open the coat and show you the rabbits that they'd poached during the night, and the rabbits would be sixpence each. So you'd select the rabbit and everybody would have rabbit dinner that day. You'd skin the rabbit and wash it in salt water and then my mother would put it on to cook. But you'd keep the skin and stuff it with newspaper and put it in the washhouse.

Betty James, born 1922

Mr and Mrs Ned One-arm

Ned One-arm and his wife would come around. He was the rag and bone man. He'd come from Cefn, and they'd got this hand-made truck with big wheels on it. He had a big, drooping black moustache and no teeth, and he always wore a big hat and he would shout, 'Rags and bones! Any rabbit skins?' His wife would be pushing the cart. She was a little round old woman, always wore a bonnet tied under her chin, and a knitted shawl over her shoulders. Of course, we used to say, 'Ned One-arm is around.' And we'd take the skins and any rags that we'd got. If you had any woollen rags, you'd get tuppence and a balloon. They'd have balloons hanging on the cart. Or she'd got parasols that she'd made out of sticks and pleated wallpaper ... if you'd got

Janet Williams' great-taid poaching up the canal with his dog and his mates. (Janet Williams)

cotton rags, you'd only get a parasol. A rabbit skin, you'd get tuppence for, and a penny for a couple of jam jars.

Betty James, born 1922

Ned Squeeze

Ned Squeeze would come from Garth and he used to sharpen shears, scissors and knives. But he was nearly always drunk. He'd come on a bike and he'd turn the bike over, to turn the grinding stone.

Betty James, born 1922

Sticky Steve and his sisters

Cecil: My uncle, they called him Sticky Steve. He was very pedantic. Well, they courted for forty-four years and then they eloped. They got married in Corwen.

Patricia: He had two very odd sisters who lived in Fron and they used to polish the coal before they put it on the fire. And every night they used to take all the silver to bed with them, in case they had a burglary. Very odd.

Cecil Diggory, born 1920, and Patricia Diggory, born 1924

Swimming in the canal

It was Peter Griffiths from the Chain Bridge who used to swim the canal to Llangollen. He used to have an oilskin thing that he would fasten round his waist and he would swim – his parents owned the Chain Bridge in Llangollen. And he would swim to Llangollen, do the shopping and walk home. There's all sorts of crazy things, when you think about it.

Patricia Diggory, born 1924

Pillar of the community

We were swimming on one occasion and it was pouring down, and our clothes were stored underneath the planks. So we thought, we may as well carry on swimming, as we're wet anyway. But we felt a bit foolish. And we saw Watkin Williams; he was the pillar of the Fron community, JP and all that sort of thing, coming along from Monsanto on his bike. So we hid under the planks. He came along, it was pouring with rain, and he put his bike up against the side, stripped off to his underpants and quickly jumped in! So we crept from under the planks and joined him. Watkin Williams! A great character.

Dennis Williams, born 1931

Robert Ferdinand Graesser

Robert Ferdinand Graesser was the originator of the large chemical plant which later became Monsanto and is now called Flexsys. Mr Graesser was a German by birth, who had trained as an industrial chemist and came to this country as a young man of nineteen, and eventually settled in the Cefn area. He wasn't naturalised until the 1870s and, that being so,

he was not allowed to own property but of course he could rent a home. On naturalisation he bought Bod Llwyd, the property near the tall narrow railway bridge leading from Newbridge to Bro Gwilym, and lived there with his family. The house opposite to Bod Llwyd – a red-brick built property called Riversdale – is a house he built as a wedding present for his daughter when she married the vicar of Rhosymedre, Mr J.W. Thomas. In 1880 Mr Graesser bought Argoed Hall in Fron for the sum of £3,750, the sale included the Hall and 56 acres of land. His chemical business was proving a great success and he made his fortune from the production of phenol and its derivatives, such as aspirin. He died in 1911. He walked from Argoed Hall to Monsanto's, was sat signing letters and collapsed and died at his desk.

Emrys Roberts, born 1922

Norman Graesser

Mr Graesser was the squire; he built the chemical works before he sold it to Monsanto in 1923 and was involved with the Wrexham lager works. His father had come from

The funeral of Robert Ferdinand Graesser, 1911. (Emrys Roberts)

Norman Graesser. (Emrys Roberts)

Walter Eddy. (Emrys Roberts)

Germany way back, during the Industrial Revolution, and came to this area eventually because there was coal in the Cefn, and then he started extracting oil from the coal for the oil lamps and all that. Then he brought in the process for making aspirin, from Germany, and it grew from there. He was good for Fron. The Mr Graesser I'm talking about is the son of the gentleman who came from Germany, Norman Graesser. I was in the church because our family worked for him in the big Hall, Argoed Hall, and if you wanted to keep your job, you really ought to go to church, not chapel. It was to your advantage. And of course they would not allow Welsh to be spoken in the Hall. I can understand that, he didn't want people talking about him behind his back.

Dennis Williams, born 1931

Generous to the village

The benefits in having the Graesser and Eddy families living in Fron were very considerable. They supported numerous organisations in the village, including all the places of worship and the school. I don't remember Robert Graesser or Walter Eddy but I well recall the former's son, Norman Graesser, coming to the school on prize-giving day to distribute prizes, which usually took the form of books. I've got one or two at home with a plate at the front for good attendance or progress etc. They were also very generous to the village and its inhabitants from a financial point of view.

Emrys Roberts, born 1922

Walter Eddy

Walter Eddy was a Cornishman who had trained as an engineer in the mines in Cornwall. He came as a young man to live in Fron at the time when the north-east Wales coalfields were being extensively developed. He also became agent for the limestone quarries at Fron and eventually became managing director of the company. In past times, quarrying and lime-burning in Fron was quite a sizeable industry. Initially, he lodged with John Edward and his family at Cysyllte Farm, which he subsequently bought and converted into a rather nice gentleman's residence known today as Fron House. This is the house close by the lift-up canal bridge at Fron.

Emrys Roberts, born 1922

Jonathan Powell, J.C. Edwards' chief engineer. (Diane Powell)

Jonathan Powell

Jonathan Powell was my great-great-grandfather and he was J.C. Edwards' chief engineer. Well, he has got a wonderful beard and I should imagine, if he was like all the Powells, he wasn't very tall either. Another intriguing thing, when he was married to his first wife, I've got a copy of their marriage certificate, he couldn't write his name, he just marked it with a cross, so I would think he was very much a self-educated man, probably with a lot of help from the chapel.

The announcement of his death, which was in the *Wrexham Advertiser*, 26 March 1904, says:

The death of Mr Jonathan Powell.
The whole district of Cefn mourns the death of one of its oldest and worthiest parishioners. Mr Jonathan Powell, of Llangollen Road, Acrefair, was a remarkable man, and knew the history of Cefn better than anyone. He was well and hearty on Thursday, when he went up to the glazed brickworks in Rhos, on business, but he caught a cold, and was confined to his bed on Monday, and died of inflammation on the lungs at about 11 o'clock on Tuesday morning at the age of 77. Mr Powell was the oldest employee of the well-known firm of J.C. Edwards, Terracotta Works, Ruabon, having been Chief Engineer there for 42 years. He was a staunch Baptist, being Senior Deacon at Seion Welsh Baptist Chapel in Cefn. He was the leading Nonconformist in the neighbourhood, and was widely known. The funeral takes place on Saturday.

He got his monument, as they say, with bells on. I used to think, when I was a little girl, it was the nearest we had, in the cemetery here, to Cleopatra's Needle. They made it in the brickworks here and obviously they made a mould to make the inscription, and it's as clear and unworn as it was in 1904.

Diane Powell, born 1946

W.G. Grace

My grandmother, she was a very healthy woman but she was taken ill at one time. Not too bad, you know, and her doctor was a Dr Salter of Chirk and they sent for him and he came in a horse and trap. And he walked in the house, with a big fellow behind him. So my grandmother said, 'Hello doctor.' So he turned to her and he said, 'You know who this is? W.G. Grace, the cricketer.' Because he was a friend of Dr Salter's. Yes, he walked in there.

Cecil Diggory, born 1920

The deacons of Seion Chapel, Cefn Mawr, with the minister in the centre, 1920s. (Mary Hughes)

Billy Meredith

My Great-Uncle Billy Meredith, the famous Welsh footballer – who played for Wales over fifty times, and for Manchester United and Manchester City – came to visit us in the Aqueduct, and he presented me with a little football. I went outside – I must have been seven or eight then – and I gave it one kick, and it went straight into the wood, Graesser's Wood, and we've never seen it again. My mother's still alive, she's ninety two, and she still reminds me of it, the ball that Uncle Bill presented to me but I lost, unfortunately, on the same day.

Dennis Williams, born 1931

Father Christmas

There was old chap living on the hill at Newbridge. Dickie Miles Jones, they called him. He lived with his wife. He talked through his nose. He was lame; he must have been getting old. He used to go to Hill Street Chapel three times every Sunday and in December the chapel would hold a bazaar and he'd always be Father Christmas. So for weeks coming up to December, he would do the shopping dressed as Father Christmas, and put the shopping in a sack, over his back. And he'd walk to Cefn, dressed like this, and of course,

Jonathan Powell's monument. (Diane Powell)

being innocent children, we thought he was Father Christmas and we used to say 'Hello, Father Christmas' to him. He'd say, 'You'll all be good children, and you'll see what I'll bring you, on Christmas Eve.'

Betty James, born 1922

Big John Jesus

The first vicar [of Rhosymedre church] was John David Edwards and it is said that he'd got such a powerful singing voice that people could hear him on a Sunday if they were on Coed Richard.

Rhona Roberts, born 1928

Robert the Rhos

Robert the Rhos was a gospel preacher and he used to preach opposite Pen-y-wal. He'd start off with two or three but maybe he'd have fifty or sixty listening at the end.

Emrys Roberts, born 1922

The Bluck boys

The Bluck boys used to live up towards Garth, the mountain, you know. But then they moved down to live in Tai Gwynedd. I knew all the Blucks. There was Bill Bluck, he was the eldest, then Jack Bluck, who became a clergyman, and George Bluck, Cyril Bluck, Sidney Bluck and Alfie Bluck. Their mam used to have a chip shop on the top of Gasworks Hill. It's down now, the shop, and that's gone now.

Betty Thompson, born 1922

The Bluck brothers

There was an old man who had his own armchair but I decided to sit on his lap and he seemed to like it. 'Oh, look at Pauline,' they all said. 'Nobody else sits on that chair.' He was one of my great-grandfathers but I found that

out years after he and the chair were gone. I never quite knew who anyone was at first, only that I had hordes of uncles and aunties, almost all of them in and out, smoking and talking at once, loud and bright as parrots. I learnt their names by being taught to pray for them, 1950s-style, 'God bless Uncle Bill and Aunty Olwen, Uncle George and Aunty Bet, Uncle Cyril and Aunty Phyllis, Uncle Sid and Aunty Win, Uncle Alf and Aunty Trudie.'

Sweet-tempered George was my Dad's best friend and he and his wife Bet, a cheerful, red-headed extrovert, stayed in touch for years, teasing me to stay proud of being Welsh, trying to help a bookish teenager have more fun. For years, George walked with a pronounced limp because he and another of my uncles [possibly Cyril] were caught in an accident in Monsanto's sometime in the 1960s in which a tank exploded, and George was by far the worst injured. Part of his treatment involved microsurgery to his head, which was a very new technique then.

I've no idea how my Dad [Jack Bluck, born 1916] progressed from an earnest lad who worked at Monsanto's, went on walking holidays and only drank water, to being an oil company worker based in Persia, with a vaguely romantic-looking Second World War passport giving him permission to travel anywhere. He was, said my Mum, the agent who was supposed to blow up the oil pipelines if the war came in their direction. He was also a bright, ordinary lad who liked the local people better than the gin-and-tonic British expats, fell in with a group of mad clergy around the cathedral who weren't snobbish in that particular way, and came home determined to be like them, despite his mother's disapproval on the grounds that clergy do no real work. Both my grandmothers died in 1969, the year I was seventeen, and my father took both their funerals.

I never knew my Grandad Bluck. I was told he started out as a miner but his health wasn't

anything much from the First World War, which my Gran found exasperating. I had thought this was shell shock but my Uncle Cyril said he had been affected by mustard gas.

After we moved away, we were treated like proper visitors [by Gran Bluck]. We had to sit in the big living room with the baize tablecloth as if we were at a funeral, and eat tinned pears with evaporated milk out of the best dishes, which I loved because we only had proper cream at home.

Cyril built their bungalow with his own hands, with help from his brothers. He was still living there when I saw him last year before his death, still showing me round the rooms with pride. I had seen it as a child, but forgotten it, and very little was changed, although he, elderly and attacked by emphysema and grief, was shrunken within it.

Pauline (Polly) Bluck, born 1952

Polly Bluck's paternal grandparents at her parents' wedding, December 1950. (Polly Bluck)

Gert's grandad

My grandad was a painter and decorator. There was a firm of him and my two uncles, in Cefn. And he always used to go and grain all the seats in the chapel, paint them and grain them. All the pubs were closed on a Sunday and my grandad used to go and do all the pubs out for them, on a Sunday.

Gertrude Jones, born 1915

Freddy Butt

After the air raids we'd have the various wardens coming round, especially one, a character in Cefn, always affectionately known as Freddy Butt, Freddy Buttington, kept a greengrocer's and sold fish in Cefn. 'Are you all right here? Do you want anything?' I don't know what they could bring, actually, but he would come to see if we were all OK. I suppose it was part of their duties.

Kathleen Smith, born 1923

Freddy Aeroplane

We used to have a guy in Fron called Freddy Aeroplane and I said to my aunt ... why was he called Aeroplane? She thinks, he always had a long raincoat and in the wind it used to flap, he never had it shut up properly, and that's why they called him Freddy Aeroplane. But he was the local journalist and he was a lovely man, soft-spoken. Freddy Jones, his real name was, but everyone knew him as Freddy Aeroplane.

Dennis Williams, born 1931

Jim Wilding

I remember one time in the foundry, there was a man called Jim Wilding working there, he moulded the castings there. And some of the hot metal got on his foot. He ran straight to the door facing the canal and he leapt, and he cleared the canal and came right to the other side. He'd have won a medal in the Olympics! I can see him now. Aye, old Jim. It burnt his shoe off and he landed on the other side. You wouldn't do it if he was normal, terrorised, I suppose.

Cecil Diggory, born 1920

Dennis Davis

He was probably one of the world's natural teachers – wonderful storyteller. I was talking to my neighbour, who also went to Acrefair School, and I said, 'Do you remember Dennis's storytelling? Do you remember Pyecraft?' 'Oh yes,' he said, 'I remember Pyecraft.' He used to tailor his stories according to the class he had and they always used to feature four children out of the class, two boys and two girls. Pyecraft was a pilot who landed on the Ballast, at Acrefair School, and these four children were playing there, and he asked them, would they like to go for a ride? So off they went with him, and when they were up in the air, they saw a strange green cloud and when they landed again, they discovered that everyone else had been turned to stone. And the story continued with how these children survived, how they found food. I don't remember it ever ending, whether it had a happy ending. It's about fifty years since I heard it!

Diane Powell, born 1946

Sally Sticks

There was an old lady come from Rhos – well, not old, old to us – and she used to sell the *Echo* and the *Sentinel*, and she'd be shouting, 'Evening *Sentinel, Echo*!' and 'Bob's your uncle!' she used to say, and she was always outside the pub, with a big bag, selling these papers.

Gertrude Jones, born 1915

The street cleaner

We used to have an old chap come with a horse and cart and brush the road and take all the weeds from the sides, and he would have a sack over his shoulders to protect him from the weather.

Betty James, born 1922

The lampman

Every night, the chap used to come from the Cefn on his bike, with a long pole, and he used to light the lamps. He used to pull the lever down to turn the gas on and then he'd come in the morning and put it off. For many years this guy was quite important, riding around on his bike, lighting the street lamps.

Dennis Williams, born 1931

nine
Musing

Eight generations

My daughter is actually the eighth generation of our family to have been born in the house. That's eight generations, a long way back. So there are lots and lots of things in the house that have been there since my great-grandad was a little boy. So it's quite nice to have all that sort of thing around you really.

Janet Williams, born 1965

There were always things happening

This area was amazing – lots of big open spaces, funny little paths and side roads like Jinny's Hill, the Rocha Steps and the Six – or, as we called them – the Thirty Nine Steps. It seemed as if every one was in a choir or a band. There were always things happening – outings, parades, gala days, chapel events

– and Cefn Mawr was full of shops. You could help on the farms and earn some extra pocket money and get milk fresh from the dairy and eggs still warm.

Sonia T. Benbow-Jones, born 1943

Nothing changes really

I had a very close friend who lived in the house just at the back of the bakehouse, so I was always up and down the steps, back and to, to see her. She had a pony on our field, so we used to take the pony all over the place. People used to come out and give us carrots. They still do, actually. When my children go out on their ponies, sometimes people will come out with a carrot or an apple. Nothing changes really, does it? It's funny, a lot of things stay the same, even though things are so different.

Janet Williams, born 1965

Places change

Places change, they say never go back, don't they?

Betty Thompson, born 1922

You just don't know

You wonder how history would have been changed and it's these small things that when you're getting older, like us, you look back and you think, 'Yes, there was a crossroads there, why didn't we do this, or why didn't we do the other?' But you just don't know, do you?

Patricia Diggory, born 1924

Days gone by

There are not many of us left now from that era but when we do meet, we talk about those days gone by.

Betty James, born 1922

Janet Williams' grandparents with her mother. (Janet Williams)

The old days

I'm glad to do this sort of thing, it revives the old days.

Cecil Diggory, born 1920

Thinking about the past

Thank you for giving me the excuse, for want of a better word, for thinking about the past.

Julie Williams, born 1954

Memory is like that

Almost all of this could be wrong, but memory is like that, isn't it? I was five when we moved away from Wales, and no longer know what I actually remember, what I picked up from somewhere, aged ten or twenty, and what has got tangled in my own mind.

Pauline (Polly) Bluck, born 1952

Janet Williams' grandfather in front of the stable where they still have horses. (Janet Williams)

The aqueduct. (Hilary Spragg)

Other local titles published by Tempus

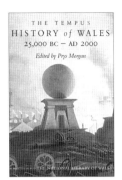

The Tempus History of Wales
PRYS MORGAN

Wales was at the heart of the Industrial Revolution, with towns like Merthyr Tydfil driving the engine of the British Empire. The cultural and social divide between modern, industrialised Wales and the traditional agricultural areas is explored within this comprehensive volume.

0 7524 1983 8

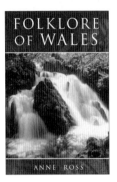

Folklore of Wales
ANNE ROSS

Wales is a Celtic country and the Celts have always treasured oral learning and recitation. Indeed they have a passion for committing facts to memory rather than relying on the written word. So it is no surprise, as we can see from Anne Ross' study, that the Welsh folklore and story-telling is so rich and varied.

0 7524 1935 8

Wrexham Football Club 1950-2000
GARETH M. DAVIES AND PETER JONES

Wrexham FC has developed into one of the most respected clubs in the Football League. Their daring deeds include reaching the quarter-finals of the English FA Cup on three occasions. The Robins' most notable achievement was their victory over Arsenal in the FA Cup in 1992. This pictorial history, which includes over 200 photographs, traces the history of the club, right up to the change of nickname, from Robins to Red Dragons, and will appeal to anyone with an interest in Wrexham Football Club.

0 7524 2400 9

The Montgomery Canal
HARRY ARNOLD

The Montgomery Canal runs through some of the most spectacular scenery in the British Isles as it crosses the border counties of England and Wales. The route passes through Shropshire and Powys as it links the Llangollen Canal at Frankton Junction with Newtown. Written by Harry Arnold, renowned waterways journalist, photographer and co-founder of the restoration scheme, this history features many photographs from his extensive archive and includes rare views of *L.T.C. Rolt's Cressy*, one of the most famous boats in waterways history.

0 7524 1660 X

If you are interested in purchasing other books published by Tempus, or in case you have difficulty finding any Tempus books in your local bookshop, you can also place orders directly through our website
www.tempus-publishing.com